Victory Lane

To order additional copies of *Victory Lane*,

by Crystal Earnhardt, call

1-800-765-6955.

Visit us at

www.reviewandherald.com

for information on other Review and Herald® products.

CRYSTAL EARNHARDT

Victory Lane

THE JOHN EARNHARDT STORY

ℝ

REVIEW AND HERALD® PUBLISHING ASSOCIATION
HAGERSTOWN, MD 21740

This book was
Edited by Jeannette R. Johnson
Cover designed by Luemas Design
Interior designed by Trent Truman
Cover photos by Corbis Images/AP/Wide World Photos
Electronic makeup by Shirley M. Bolivar
Typeset: 10/14 Bookman

PRINTED IN U.S.A.

07 06 05 04 03   5 4 3 2 1

R&H Cataloging Service
Earnhardt, Crystal Jolene
    Race to victory lane: The John Earnhardt story.

    1. Earnhardt, John R.   I. Title

                    B

ISBN 0-8280-1723-9

Dedication

To my husband, John,

who is the kindest man I know.

Without his experiences and spiritual leadership,

this book couldn't have been written.

And to my children—

Angie, Tammy, and Carrie.

Introduction

We spend our years as a tale that is told. . . .

So teach us to number our days, that we may

apply our hearts unto wisdom.

—PSALM 90:9-12

It has been joked that NASCAR began on the Southern back roads that led from one dry county to the next. There, bootleggers hauled their beer and liquor in various disguises. Cases of whiskey stored neatly beneath bins of corn, potatoes, or bales of hay in the back of their trucks made their way to consumers. Some went so far as to use their smiling or sleeping children as decoys. What law officer would search the seat or bed of a child?

The "respectable" bootleggers were horrified at such sneakiness. Why, if they weren't faster than the law, then they ought to find another trade! They artfully rebuilt the springs in their vehicles so the law couldn't detect a heavier load. Then they added a toggle switch under the dash so they could turn off their taillights during a chase. That made it easier to change roads without being detected. The really clever bootleggers mounted a small white light under their front bumper that would follow the centerline in the road, and then they wouldn't have to use their lights at all. So began the chase across fields, roads, and waterways—the law hotly pursuing the lawless.

Eventually the law realized it was a lost cause. Moonshiners and bootleggers far outweighed their tiny forces. Besides, the taxpayers couldn't afford to keep buying new cars for their sheriffs. Better for them to legalize the stuff. At least it would knock the bootleggers out of business.

The bootleggers, on the other hand, had fallen in love with the fast cars and juiced-up engines. To them, racing was far more fun than any known sport. NASCAR may not totally agree with this entire story, but the fact remains that many of the early drivers really began as bootleggers and alcohol suppliers. They have been—and still are—major sponsors.

Evil angels have had their day basking in success; however, God's love for the poor staggering souls who drink Satan's poison has never ceased. He sent His Son to die for them. This book is powerful proof that He still reaches down among the grease pits of sin.

Sometimes He sends an angel. . . . In this case He sent a nurse.

Ruth never fully comprehended the significance of her prayer that morning in the bootlegger's shanty. As she and her husband, Dr. Oliver, drove into the hard-packed dirt frontage that served as the parking lot of the Veteran's Grill, she recoiled in disapproval. The crude building had once been two Army barracks that had been hooked together, forming an L-shaped structure. The front part was the grill where the owners, Julia and James Earnhardt, served sandwiches and beer. The second barracks was their living quarters.

James, a quiet man everyone knew as Shorty, stood out front, waiting to direct them to his wife, who was in the last stages of labor. Like all new fathers, he seemed relieved that help had finally arrived. After a brief hello, he hurried them around the side of the building. Ruth vaguely noticed the beer advertisements decorating the windows as she sidestepped puddles that had been created from the recent spring rain. Two small dark-haired girls and a boy stopped their play in the backyard to eye her curiously.

Ruth smiled and waved at them. She had once promised God that she would treat all people with dignity. It didn't matter to her if their patients were poor farmers, rich business-people, or even families living in the back of a tavern. They were all God's children, though some didn't know it yet.

But this delivery was somewhat different from the hundreds that Dr. Oliver attended to each year. Ten miles away a little girl played by herself while her mother looked on in silent sadness. The girl had been told that her daddy was dead, but nurse Ruth knew he wasn't dead. He was the man who was now urging them toward a back bedroom.

A few years earlier Ruth had been present at the delivery of this woman's other children—the dark-haired girls and the boy playing in the yard—while her previous husband was away in the Army. Mixed-up lives. Broken hearts. Sometimes it made her sick. She hated knowing all the dark secrets of the people she served. Forcing herself, she smiled cheerfully as she entered the dimly lit bedroom.

"Good morning, Julia. How do you feel?"

"Not good right now." Julia sighed with relief at the sight of help. "I'm hurting right bad."

Dr. Oliver wasted no words as he washed his hands, then flipped back the covers to examine her. He had left a waiting room full of patients, some of whom were coughing and burning with fever. He hated to do that, but what choice did he have? Babies chose the most inappropriate times to make their entrance into the world. With the shortage of doctors in Rowan County, he'd just have to do the best he could. He knew that Julia didn't have long labors.

Working beside him, Ruth busied herself bathing the patient's face with a cool cloth and preparing clean sheets and towels for the delivery. As she hurried back and forth between the kitchen sink and the bedroom, she couldn't help wondering what the other half of the building where Julia served the customers was like. For sure, it wasn't your ordinary all-American home. She knew the jokes and coarse laughter that resonated off those walls. She had sewed up wide-open gashes from the fights that were the result of alcohol and attended the funerals of those who never made it home because of bleary eyes and poor judgment.

And now this innocent baby was arriving in this place. Pity welled up within her. How would God judge the children who came from such an environment?

A pain-ridden scream and a final push sent the infant sliding out of the womb, fists curled in anger, mouth wide open. Dr. Oliver cut and clamped the umbilical cord and handed the baby to Ruth. She moved with practiced skill, quickly suctioning out the small mouth.

Lord, she prayed silently, *may he learn words of praise to You.* As she cleaned out his ears she thought of the ugly words that he would soon hear. *May he hear Your voice when You speak, dear*

Lord. With a clean cloth she wiped the corner of the eyes in gentle outward movements. *May he see with his heart, Lord.* Then she bathed the blood and vernix off his body. *May his hands do Your bidding. May his feet walk in Your paths.*

"What are you going to name him?" Dr. Oliver asked the tired mother.

"John," Julia answered.

Dr. Oliver chuckled. "I should have guessed. Let's see; you have Judy, Jean, Jimmy, and now a Johnny."

"My father's name is John," she said, "and both of my husbands' names begin with J."

Ruth cuddled the baby close to her and looked into his dark-blue eyes. "So your name is John. That's good. It means 'traveler for God.'"

Dr. Oliver cleared his throat. Ruth had learned through the years that he automatically did that when he was ready to leave. "Are you almost finished?" he asked. "I think the papa is anxiously waiting to see his son."

She could see a large shadow looming just beyond the bedroom door. The man stepped into the light, then paused, waiting for an invitation to enter. Three grimy faces peered around his legs.

Ruth smiled down at the children. "I want each of you to wash your hands very clean before you touch your brother."

All four of them disappeared without a word. Ruth reluctantly wrapped a blanket around the baby. There was nothing more she could do. She couldn't make his parents change. She couldn't tuck the little tyke into bed each night and tell him Bible stories. Only God could pluck a brand from the burning. To Him she must commit this babe.

Reverently she lifted him up and concluded her silent prayer. *Dear Lord, please bless this child. Protect him from this environment, and somehow use him so that he can grow up to be of service to You. Make him a traveler for You.*

It was a simple, heartfelt prayer. How could she know that God would answer her petition in a way beyond her wildest dreams?

Chapter 2

Julia slapped six slices of bread, side by side, on the counter. Next she speared sliced ham and dropped it on the bread. She grabbed the mustard and, with one continuous squeeze, dribbled it on each sandwich.

"Getting mighty hungry out here!" a loudmouthed weasel of a man bellowed. "Can I come back there and help you, darlin'?"

"You won't walk out of here alive if you do," Julia shot back. "I'm dangerous with a knife." She put a sandwich on a saucer and grabbed a frosty mug out of the cooler, filling it to overflowing with cold, frothy beer. A sly smile curved her lips as she turned and placed it gently on the serving counter. "How's your wife, Jed? I haven't seen her lately."

"That's why I come here," he grinned at her. "If I drink enough beer I can't see her either." He laughed out loud at his own joke.

The man beside him spoke up. "My wife's so big nothin' can blur her from my sight." He leaned across the counter and spoke confidentially. "I'd like something a little stronger, if you don't mind, sweetheart."

Julia looked around. "You know it's illegal to serve whiskey over the counter."

"Shucks, ain't nobody here but Jed and me," he wheedled. "Who's gonna know?"

"Well, supposin' the sheriff walks in?"

"Iffen he does, I'll accidentally spill it on your side of the counter. Now hurry up! My honey gets mean when I don't get home on time."

Julia stood her ground. "I don't keep whiskey in the store," she said.

Bud was getting ugly. She could see his face turning redder than usual. His knuckles clenched the mug. Some people turned mean and demanding after drinking a few beers. There was no reasoning with them. Others turned the exact opposite and became silly and agreeable. She had dealt with them all. Bud was about to argue with her when the tavern door opened and two construction workers came in and took seats by the window.

"What can I get you?" she called out, relieved for the interruption.

"A couple burgers to go—and a Coke," one of them answered.

As Julia fried the burgers, she wondered absently what her kids were doing. They'd been awfully quiet. She really ought to fix them a good supper tonight. Little Johnny had complained that he was tired of ham sandwiches and burgers. Maybe she could mash some potatoes and toss a salad. She grimaced at the thought of more cooking. Her shoulders and legs ached from standing all day. A long hot soak in the bathtub would be so wonderful. If only Mama were here to help watch after them.

A tear slid down her cheek. Dear old Mama. How she missed her. Why did she die? Didn't God know how much she had depended on her? She flipped the burgers, mayonnaised the bread, and reached for the onion and pickles. Mama had died holding her hand. Diabetes had triumphed at last. "I love you, Sissy," she had said. Those were her last words.

The door rattled again, and in walked a tall, thin man with a thick head of white hair. She looked up from her work and smiled at him. "Hi, Pop."

Her father beamed at her. "Hey, Sis! How are you?"

"Tired." She poured the construction workers' Cokes and carried them to the counter. "Burgers are ready," she called out.

Her father looked around. "Where's James?"

She could see his hands shaking. She knew why he had come, and it angered her. He knew she wouldn't give him a drink—but James would. And he wouldn't leave until he had one.

"You know what the doctor said, Pop. You're gonna die if you don't quit."

"I'm gonna die either way, Sis. I haven't slept for two days.

Just let me have a little to calm my nerves. I've got to get some relief."

He was begging. She hated to see her father this way, and yet she understood how the craving for alcohol became so strong that a body yearned for drink more than food. She had seen alcoholics steal their families' grocery money and leave little children at home hungry in order to satisfy that thirst. Deep down she knew her father was unable to quit, short of being bound and tied to a chair. He would get that drink somehow. Still, loyalty toward her mother prevented her from moving an inch.

"He's in the back, Pop," she sighed.

"Thank ya, Sissy." He spoke her nickname softly and hurried around the counter.

The construction workers paid for their food, then stepped outside and lit cigarettes.

Bud scowled and tossed some money on the counter. "Come on, Jed," he said loudly. "There are other places besides this one."

Julia leaned against the counter and watched them leave. It had been a long day, and she was tired. Her feet ached, her back hurt. Mentally she pictured the mounds of dirty laundry that waited for her attention. There seemed to be no rest in sight.

Her father returned with a new bounce in his step. He smiled and patted her on the back. "I'll see you later," he said. She started to follow him out the door, but he objected. "No. Go prop your feet up while you can. I'm all right now."

As she turned and headed back to the kitchen the sight of Johnny passing by the window made her think of mashed potatoes. "Wait, Pop!" she yelled as she made an about-face and ran out the door. "Come back in about an hour for sup—" The word died in midair as she saw beyond her father to the woman who was waiting for him in the car.

How could he bring another woman on her property? How dare he! Prop her feet up indeed! He hadn't been thinking of her at all. He was hiding the truth from her, using her just as he had used Mama. Anger boiled up within her, crowding out any reason. She dashed to the car, shouting obscenities at him, and then turned on the horror-stricken woman whose mouth was hanging open almost to her chest.

"How dare you sit in my mama's seat!" she screamed. "The grass hasn't even covered her grave yet." When she jerked the car door open, the frightened woman attempted to get out the other side, but Julia crawled in after her. She grabbed her by the hair and jerked her out on the ground, bashing her head against the car door. She slapped her face again and again, screaming horrible names. At last, exhausted, she dropped her and turned to her father, who stood frozen on the spot. Behind him, the construction workers made a dash to their truck and pulled out fast.

"Don't you ever bring another woman on my property again!" she shouted at her father. "Do you understand me?"

He nodded, and without saying a word he lifted the bleeding woman off the ground and shoved her into the car. He ran to the other side, faster than Julia had ever seen him move. In his haste he put the car in drive, almost hitting the building before he realized his error. Jerking it into reverse, he spun out of the dirt parking lot.

Shocked at her own behavior and at his fright of her, Julia almost laughed in spite of her tears. As she turned she saw Johnny standing there, wide-eyed. He moved back in fear as she approached him. "What do you want, Johnny?" she demanded, struggling to regain her composure.

The boy hung his head, afraid to look in her eyes.

"Well, what is it?" she demanded. "What do you want?" If there was one child who tried her patience, it was this one.

"I was hungry and wanted to know what we were having for supper," he said, not much louder than a whisper.

Suddenly she had no strength left. Rubbing her aching head with one hand, she opened the door and flipped over the "closed" sign. She couldn't even think of cooking. Not now. "I've got some nice ham sandwiches already made." She tried to sound cheerful. "Come on in, and I'll get you a pickle and some Coke to go with it."

ames Earnhardt slammed the phone down hard, the words echoing in his head. "The bears will be out tonight!" Tonight of all nights! There was no doubt as to the meaning. He had 10 cases of beer sitting in his basement, waiting to be delivered just across the county line. He thanked the good laws of Stanley County that no alcoholic beverages be sold within its borderlines. That made less competition for him. Living three miles outside of the border made it real easy to slip in and out and make some easy money.

He wondered how the police had gotten wind of the party that was to take place on such a respectable day. They must have bribed some drunken idiot last night. He stroked his chin and walked to the window. The bright morning sunshine almost hurt his eyes. He could hear shouts of laughter as two little heads bobbed around the corner of the house, one child in hot pursuit of the other. But his thoughts were far from his children. *Who was the informer?* Well, one thing was certain. They knew only that there was to be a party. The location had been abruptly changed to protect any attendees. He'd have to take a back road. No, on second thought, the law would have those roads covered.

Had James been paying attention, he would have noticed that Johnny was brandishing a stick over Jean's head. And he might have noticed that his neighbors were coming out of their house in their Sunday morning best. No doubt on their way to church. As they neared the family car the two children, followed closely by their barking dog, reversed directions. Now Johnny was screaming and Jean had the stick.

Jean must have caught up with Johnny, because he ran up

the steps, crying and clutching his face that now sported a long red welt about the size of a stick. Those two roughneck kids were enough to make a preacher swear! He smiled, remembering that the whole church could attest to that fact.

That's when the answer hit him like an unsuspecting branch when you're walking in the woods and think you've got your head bent down low enough. *The kids!* Their darling little cherub faces and rosy cheeks . . . . Nobody could resist the smile that Jean flashed, or Johnny's big Carolina blue eyes. At least no stranger could. Anybody would have to know them for a day or so before they became hardened to their childish charms.

James laughed out loud. It certainly wasn't a new trick. No, indeed! But it would work. He knew it would—especially in broad daylight.

Grabbing his car keys, he hurried to open the door just as Johnny reached it on the other side. "Hey, sport!" He smiled and patted the tear-stained cheeks. "Jean bashed you good, didn't she? When you play with fire, son, you're gonna git burned. I warned you about getting rough with her. Now git inside to your mama. She'll fix you up."

Johnny stopped crying as his father fairly danced down the steps. "Where are you going, Daddy?"

"Well, you and Jean and your mama and me are going to take a little ride this afternoon. I've got to get the car packed and make you and Jean a nice soft bed in the back."

"But I'm not tired, Daddy. I don't want to go to bed!"

"We're not leaving for a while. You'll be tired by the time we do. Now run inside and get dressed in your Sunday best."

He drove the station wagon to the basement door to load the cargo. Speaking of Sunday best, what a good idea! Should he wear his black suit? Maybe even put a Bible on the seat. Just an average family going out for a ride after church. He began to whistle, and then laughed out loud as he thought of the police sitting on the back roads in the dark, waiting for a dirty old bootlegger.

Chapter 4

*T*he delivery was a cinch. Four men met them in an alley parking lot and unloaded the car. Within minutes they were on their way home, pockets bulging with cash.

"Easiest money I ever made," James grinned at his radiant wife. "I think we all deserve a treat."

"Like what, Daddy?" Johnny asked.

"Ice cream?" Jean asked hopefully.

James turned the car into the parking lot of a busy restaurant. "Let's stop at the diner and get some roast and mashed potatoes." He winked at Jean. "Then we'll have ice cream for dessert."

"What about Judy and Jimmy?" Johnny wanted to know. "You left them at home."

"We'll take a plate to them," his mother answered. "Now, don't you worry none about them. They stayed at home to give us more room. You can have a double helping of mashed potatoes. You and Jean were so good back there on your beds. You helped us get our work done."

Mashed potatoes! And all they had to do was lie quietly in the back of the station wagon. What a perfect day!

As the two children ate, James smoked a cigarette and leaned back. "I want to open a racetrack, Julia," he announced.

"Get out of here!" She laughed and poked him on the arm. "Where would we put a racetrack?"

"About a mile back through the woods, behind the house." He took a napkin and began drawing a map, pinpointing the exact location. "I'm serious. It's an easy way to earn some bucks. It would be a lot of fun, too. I bet the whole town of Gold Hill would come, and half of the county too. You could sell hot dogs, popcorn, and drinks. That alone would bring in some good bucks."

"What brought this up?"

James crushed his cigarette and dropped the butt on his plate. "It won't be long before they legalize alcohol in every county. Right now we're fairly safe, but it won't last."

"But we have the Grill, and you're doing good with the trucking."

"We're in a rut. We need some excitement."

"I think you've got more nerve than brains," Julia commented.

Johnny watched as his mother struggled with the idea. Every time she came up with an objection, Dad came up with an answer. He and Jean finally lost interest and happily licked their cones. The discussion continued all the way home, with Dad consistently gaining ground.

Unknown to Johnny, another little boy by the name of Dale Earnhardt sat in the next county listening to similar discussions around his table. His father, Ralph, didn't particularly want a track in his backyard; he just wanted to be driving the fastest car around the tracks, wherever they might be. His wife worried about his safety, worried about the money, and just plain worried. Both women knew their life was about to change. They just had no idea how much.

Chapter 5

▰▰▰▰▰▰▰▰▰▰▰▰▰▰▰▰▰▰▰▰▰

he racetrack moved quickly from being a dream to becoming a reality. For months the whole family listened to the distant hum of a bulldozer about a half mile through the woods behind the house. Day after day it dug the red clay dirt and packed it into a solid track. Then came the roar of dump trucks hauling in more loads of dirt. Soon the bleachers were built; then the concession stand and the announcer's box.

In the evenings James and Kenny Wiggins from Mooresville (who would eventually become a driver for one of James's cars) revved their engines and drove round and round on the hard-packed earthen track in preparation for the races to come. The whole family stood in the bleachers to cheer the drivers on. Their voices grew hoarse and flying dust choked them.

"We've got to do something about the dust," Julia complained. "The cars kick up so much that we can't even see you out there!"

"You think you've got it bad!" James replied as he mopped his grimy face with his handkerchief. "There were times I couldn't even see the track. We'll wet it down about an hour before the race." He held out the once-white handkerchief for her to see. It was the color of red clay.

At last the opening day arrived. The children were so excited they could almost eat that dust for breakfast rather than sit in the kitchen trying to swallow rice and eggs. About an hour before the race an old creaky truck with a rusty 300-gallon tank lumbered out on the track and stopped. A man jumped from the cab and attached a long pipe with holes punched into it to the tank. The pipe hung horizontally, suspended about six inches from the ground. After a few minutes the man climbed back into the truck and started driving slowly around the track. Water poured from the holes and doused the dirt. The track immediately looked darker.

Johnny stood transfixed by the whole scene before him. The watering truck, the crowds of people climbing up the bleachers for seats, the small cars with their loud motors, the smell of damp earth and ethanol . . . It was big—bigger than he had imagined! So big the local rescue squad truck was parked on the side for emergencies, and some of their men were selling tickets. The logo on their caps and shirts read "Rowan County Rescue Squad" and could easily identify them. And to think that it was all because of his dad! Somehow the thought made him feel a little bigger, a little more important.

Other children had tagged along with their parents. A number of boys about his age hung around, watching the drivers getting ready. One of those boys was Dale Earnhardt. Johnny and Dale would find out that they had much in common. At the time they didn't know how their lives were related; all they knew was that they were only one year apart in age. They both had brown hair and blue eyes. They both shared the same last name. And at the moment, they were so excited that they were about to burst.

Chapter 6

From the day it opened until the day it closed, life for the Earnhardt family revolved around the racetrack. It became the focal point for many of the townspeople as well. Men from miles away came to see some action, tinker with motors, and drive their frustrations away. Teenage boys liked to hang out in the infield and dream about the day when they, too, could look cool while zooming in circles with the wind blowing their faces. Girls sat in the bleachers to watch the boys. Women sometimes gathered around the concession stand to watch their menfolk, or, as Julia aptly put it, "to check up on them."

The only ones who spoke out against the track were the pastors of the local Baptist and Methodist churches. While neither could boast of having more than 50 parishioners on an average Sunday, the track could honestly calculate several hundred.

Grandma Earnhardt, a thin lady with silvery, straight short hair, sided with the pastors and urged her son to open the track on Saturdays only. Johnny heard them discussing it one evening in the den.

"You were raised attending Sunday school and doing what is right," she said firmly. "Do you honestly think that betting and competing against each other is what the Lord would have you do on His holy day? This foolhearty business is going to leave your children fatherless."

"Now, Mama, I am fully convinced that the Lord will honor your prayers and keep me safe," James joked as he patted her on the knee.

Grandma wasn't amused. There were tears in her eyes as she twisted the hankerchief in her hands. "First your sister, and now you. I can't imagine what I did wrong."

"Mom, Jeanette goes to church every week!"

"But it's not on Sunday," she said sorrowfully.

Grandpa, a stout man with only an inch or two of white hair around the base of his head, cleared his throat and announced that it was time to go home. No one wanted to hear more about the sister who took Bible studies from Dr. Oliver and then began going to church on Saturday. And if that wasn't bad enough, she packed her bags and caught a train to Tennessee to attend one of the seventh-day colleges when there was a perfectly good Methodist college not more than a mile beyond their house. Grandma had dreamed of the day when her only daughter would stand on that spacious green lawn under the huge oaks and receive her diploma. No, it would do no good to bring up that subject.

Grandma dabbed at her eyes and stood up. "Well, I've had my say on the subject. It's your life. Just remember the children." She looked evenly at James. "They deserve to have a daddy."

Everyone stood by the window and watched them leave.

"I'm just trying to figure out if your dad agrees with her, or if he'd rather be at the races," Julia commented. "You know he sits in his easy chair all Sunday afternoon, reading. I couldn't stand it. It's quiet as a tomb in their house."

James said nothing as he put on his cap and headed for the basement to work on one of the cars. But if the truth be told, he thought a little of that peace and quiet would be nice occasionally.

■ ■ ■

The Earnhardt racetrack wasn't the only one enjoying success in the area. Small tracks popped up within miles of each other. Most of the others operated on Friday nights and Saturdays, allowing the drivers the opportunity to win at several different locations each weekend. Very few drivers were able to quit their full-time jobs.

NASCAR drivers were the exception. Although it began in the late 1940s, NASCAR quickly drew national attention. Most of their races were on Saturdays and used modified cars. That made it easy for some of the "greats" to visit the smaller tracks and even alternate between stock car racing and micro-midget racing.

Ralph Earnhardt often came down on Sundays to enjoy the micro-midget races and chat with his friends. He was a tall, lean man of few words, but truly a master mechanic. He had won the Grand National Championship and captured the NASCAR sportsman championship in 1956 when he won the track titles at 11 different speedways, ranging from Pennsylvania to Florida to Tennessee. His success at the Hickory, North Carolina, track was so predictable that the attendance dropped. Rumor had it that the owners promised him the winner's purse if he would just hang back and let someone else come in first. No one could have known as he hovered over the little micro-midgets on that small out-of-the-way track, offering advice and lending a helping hand, that one day his son would follow in his steps and become known as the Intimidator. To them, Dale was the son of a great driver who stood on the sidelines with the other kids and dreamed of the day when he could drive a car fast like his father.

But Dale wasn't the only child with stars in his eyes. Who could have guessed that another little boy, standing on the sidelines watching his father and uncle race micro-midgets, would become known in NASCAR as "Chocolate Myers"? He would become a valuable teammate to the Intimidator, supplying his car with gas.

No, these men had no way of knowing that they were rearing a future generation of NASCAR greats. As they huddled in little groups, discussing an exciting win or a death-defying wreck, the boys hid in the bushes nearby so they could hear their stories firsthand—not the later tamed-down version reserved for the women and children.

At the moment, the men were discussing the story of how the great Fireball Roberts missed his plane connection and was late for one of the Grand National races in Concord. This particular race was 100 miles on a half-mile dirt track. Ralph Earnhardt subbed in Fireball's place, hoping to make a win, but instead went over a dirt embankment in the 167th lap.

Most of them shook their heads or groaned in sympathy for his stroke of bad luck. Others were quick to point out that at least he wasn't hurt. A few laughed out loud. Ralph laughed with them.

Then the talk turned to the final Grand National race held at Daytona Beach. About 35,000 turned out to the farewell Beach Road event. Two men, Turner and Goldsmith, were locked in a ferocious duel for top honors when Turner spun out into the ocean, allowing Goldsmith a 10-second lead. But the ending caught everyone off guard as Goldsmith, who had lost the use of his windshield wipers, sped past the north turn on the final lap and drove up the beach.

Some of the men laughed at how surprised Goldsmith must have felt when he discovered that he was driving up the beach alone, until the storyteller, a wiry man with nails as black as grease, described how the undaunted Indianapolis 500 veteran realized his mistake and quickly cut a 180-degree turn. He then proceeded not only to catch back up but to cross the finish line a few feet ahead of the speeding Turner.

By now everyone was laughing and slapping their knees in admiration. That's how races were, surprise ending after surprise ending. Some lost in spite of how hard they tried. Others won through sheer determination, skill, and a stroke of good fortune. And then some won by illegally alternating car parts or getting through a faulty scorekeeping system.

The boys' interest began to wane when the talk turned to scorekeeping problems. Apparently one of the most controversial events in the history of NASCAR Grand National racing had just taken place. Lee Petty was declared the winner of a 100-mile race, according to the scorecards. The only problem was that his competitor, Curtis Turner, claimed "that Mama Elizabeth (Petty's wife and scorekeeper) had the fastest pencil in NASCAR."

The race was so close that there was a doubt as to which team led the most laps. Turner called up Bill France, who was the head of NASCAR, and demanded a new and more accurate method of keeping score.

And so it went, week after week. Excitement. Fast cars. Fast money. A rush of adrenaline. Some gaining wealth. Others losing everything.

Meanwhile, two little boys stood close by with stars in their eyes, watching their heroes speeding in the fast lane. It was an image they would never forget, and for one of the boys a legacy that would chart his life's course.

Chapter 7

Johnny felt that if he lived to be 100 he still would never be able to understand his oldest sister, Judy. She loved twirling the baton around like a drum major while looking at herself in the mirror. She took control of the whole house when Mom was working and bossed everybody else as though they were her servants. As far as Johnny was concerned, Judy had either let the baton hit her head one too many times, or he had an alien for a stepsister.

He was too young and immature at the time to comprehend that a stepchild might feel a bit misplaced. After all, his mom was *his* mom, and his dad was *his* dad. Mom was Judy's mom, but dad was the man who moved in when her dad moved away. At that time Judy was too young to understand the complications of a marriage gone sour but old enough to miss her father, who went back to New York and was seldom heard from again.

Maybe, in her childish mind, she felt as though she had done something wrong that had caused Daddy to go away. Maybe she just plain resented another man taking her daddy's place so quickly. Whatever the reason, Judy kept an invisible wall between herself and her stepfather until she was about 13 years old. Though he certainly had his faults, such as drinking every other weekend, never kissing them good night, and never saying "I love you," he did provide them all with a comfortable house and plenty of food, clothes, and toys. And he never beat them or bought something for one that he didn't buy for the others.

Somehow the kids always knew that in spite of his gruffness or illegal activities, they could mostly depend on him. While he was an occasional drinker on the weekends, Julia was a consistent one. She seldom missed an opportunity to get together with her brother, Uncle J.P., and pass the bottle around. When that happened, James always got up early the next morning and cooked enough rice and eggs for the kids. "You can skip any meal but breakfast," he always told them.

The other kids worked hard every Father's Day to make or buy a present for Dad. But not Judy. She stood around watching as James oohed and aahed at the handkerchiefs Jean usually gave him and the socks that Johnny always bought. Once Jean asked Judy what she had gotten for Dad. She only tossed her head defiantly and said, "He's not my father."

After that James went out of his way to do things for Judy. His latest gesture of goodwill toward her was to pronounce her the racetrack queen. Judy wore a fancy dress and a tiara on her head like a girl would wear to a high school prom. After the announcer declared the winner of a race, Judy handed him the trophy and kissed him. Johnny guessed it made her feel important, but he felt sorry for the winner who had to stand there and smile through it.

One Sunday afternoon Johnny and the other boys gathered around the track as close as safety permitted. The trial races were over, and it was time for the main event. The drivers lined up according to the points they received in the trial race.

A thrill rushed through the crowd as the announcer bellowed over the loud speaker, "Gentlemen, start your engines!" The cars drove slowly in perfect order for the trial lap. Then the flagman lowered the green flag, and the rest of the race was the roar of engines and flying dust. Around and around the track they went. First one would lead, another would pass, and then someone would spin out, cheered on by shouting people eating popcorn and hotdogs and drinking sodas.

And then it happened. Number 25 decided to pass James on the inside of the track, but unknowingly got too close. Tire bumped tire as they approached the curve. Suddenly James's car was spinning out of control, right in the path of the rest of the drivers. Some veered off the track and into the infield to avoid hitting him. Others tried to judge the direction he was spinning to go around him, but it was too late. One car after another knocked him around until one clipped him at the back and flipped his car into the air.

Everyone watched in horror as the car's gas tank burst into flames and the vehicle landed with a thud upside down and rolled over several times. Smoke now mingled with dust in a thick haze. The rescue squad was on the track within moments, though it seemed like an eternity to those who stood frozen in the bleachers.

Johnny could see men running to the burning flames and trying to pull his dad out, but Dad wasn't moving—and the fire was too hot to linger. He vaguely heard a woman screaming, "He's gonna burn! He's burning alive!" It felt like a nightmare when a person wakes up but is unable to move or breathe. Only this was for real.

Johnny began running toward the now-still form. His legs felt like lead; he felt as if he were in slow motion. A familiar voice passing him jarred his senses. It was Judy, sailing down the track like a deer in flight, skirt flying and tiara forgotten.

"That's my daddy!" she screamed. "That's my daddy!"

The crowd held its breath as several men tried unsuccessfully to pull James from the flaming inferno. Just when all seemed hopeless, a man was seen running down the track, swinging a machete. Within minutes the safety belts were slashed in two, and James was carried to the waiting rescue squad. Sirens wailed as they rushed him away.

Everything had happened so fast. Johnny and Jean stared as their mom handed the baby to Pearly, their closest neighbor, and fled to the waiting rescue van. She didn't need to explain. Everyone knew that she had to be with her husband.

As soon as the track was cleared, the race continued. The drivers seemed to be a lot less daring, the crowd less enthusiastic. Judy, forgetting that she was supposed to give the winner a trophy and a kiss, retrieved the baby from Pearly and herded the rest of them back to the house.

"We need to stay by the phone," she said quietly. "Mama will call."

Johnny stared at her. Was this the same girl who, minutes before, had outrun him and outscreamed him all the way to the track? How could she be so hysterical one minute and so totally calm the next? He didn't dare question her. Instinctively he knew that beneath her calm external laid a firebomb waiting to go off. Even Baby Rondy lay still in her arms without a whimper. Together they walked home.

The house was quiet, so quiet that Johnny could hear the clock ticking on the mantle. He heard the people down at the track, cheering. Knowing that the race must be over, he went to the window and watched as the cars filed down the lane.

He remembered a saying his teacher once quoted when he was late for class: "Time and tide wait for no man." She then explained that time doesn't stop for anything or anybody. But as Johnny watched the clock, it seemed to be standing still. Would Mama never call?

An eternity later Mom and Dad appeared. "He's fine," Julia reassured them as she walked in the house. "A bit bruised, a few burns—but he is fine."

James brushed off their concerns. He ruffled their hair, got a drink, and then meandered out to assess the damage to his car. Terrified that he might collapse at any minute, Johnny followed him all the way to the track. He watched as his father stared at the heap of charred metal. "Somebody up there was watching over me today," he muttered.

The next week was busy as James and his neighbor, Bill, worked on the car. All the kids were so glad to have their father alive that they willingly offered to help, and together they got it repaired in time for Sunday's race. The crowd cheered madly as James drove number 00 ("Double Aught") to the starting line. And that week he won. Judy proudly walked in the winner's circle. She gave James a hug and kiss as she handed the trophy to him.

Johnny realized that something major had happened to Judy and to his father the day of the accident. It wasn't something that could be measured with a stick or noticed by a stranger. It dealt with the heart. Somehow they developed a new understanding and respect for each other. You might call it love between a daughter and her stepfather. It was a great discovery.

Chapter 8

Besides having the races on Sunday afternoons, Johnny had another reason for loving that day. The law required that on Sundays the Grill that his mom and dad owned and operated beside the house had to be closed. No beer or alcoholic beverages could be sold on the day that most people in the community deemed holy.

Sometimes his mom insisted they all go to Sunday school, such as the time the superintendent had promised a special pin for those with perfect attendance for a year. For some reason earning that pin meant a great deal to Mom. So week after week they attended.

However, the Saturday night parties in the basement or the Grill never ended until the wee hours of the morning. More often than not Mom and Dad were suffering from a headache and couldn't get up in time. While they slept it off, Johnny and his sister Jean would get in their own micro-midgets and race around the Grill parking lot, or practice leg races on the track. Jean was a daredevil and agile as a cat. She could lie on her stomach and touch her head with her feet. She could outrun and outrace most boys her age, or even older.

Then one Saturday night something so disturbing happened that neither one of them felt like racing or playing games of any kind. It was so bad that Johnny had to get away to sort things out. He grabbed his fishing pole and headed down to Greer's pond.

Greer's pond was the local hangout for the neighborhood boys. It was nothing more than a large pond in the middle of a field, with just enough trees for shade, just enough blackberry bushes to provide a healthful snack during the summer, and just enough brim and crappie to make fishing a challenge.

To get to the pond, John had to walk down the road and through a large patch of woods, a quiet and peaceful walk. Ordinarily the boy would have been more aware of the birds flitting among the trees or the rabbits that stood perfectly still until he came within a foot of them. But this day his thoughts were so preoccupied with the events of the previous night that he could think of little else. Perhaps the serenity of nature would calm his still shaking hands.

He stood on the bank, baited his hook, and slung it in. Once the fishing line was in the water, he glanced around out of habit to make sure no one was looking. Then he reached into his pocket and pulled out a cigarette. He lit it and took a long drag.

Mom and Dad had forbidden him to smoke anymore. He thought that was quite hypocritical since they had permitted customers to put him on the counter in the Grill when he was little and had put cigarettes in his mouth. He learned a few jokes to make it comical and send the most sober man into fits of laughter. Of course, he was supposed to hold the cigarette with his lips, not actually smoke it. But what difference did it make? Dad smoked, and Mama dipped. He breathed in the tobacco fumes secondhand anyway. Besides, if they were so concerned about his personal well-being, it certainly hadn't shown last night.

Thoughts of last night made him close his eyes to shut out the fear.

Problems began after Dad drove the station wagon to the basement door. A phone call interrupted, warning him of law enforcement on the lookout. Still, he loaded the boxes of alcoholic beverages to be delivered to a private party in the next county.

"I'm going to need the kids tonight," he told Julia. "Judy and Jimmy are too big, but John and Jean are still short enough to make good decoys."

It had been some time since either one of them had been used as decoys. When they were younger they didn't understand their part in the bootlegging operation. It was just a matter of going to sleep while out for a ride. But now that he was older Johnny didn't like it one bit, and being described as short added insult to injury.

Mom had always told him that boys sprouted taller when they be- came teenagers. He still had a couple years to go. The added dis- comfort of hard boxes for a bed made him less willing.

"Now, Johnny"—Mom tried to soothe things over by using her sugary voice usually reserved for strangers—"you'll be getting paid for this job. Aren't you saving up for a new bike?"

John squinted up at her. He had been saving up for a new bike for a long time, one that had high, silver handlebars; a long blue, vinyl banana seat; a large, black, knobby, back tire; and blue sparkle metallic paint. He had wanted it ever since he saw it parked outside the Carolina Tire Company. The promise of money made the bike seem a reality. He could almost see it in the garage, parked beside Dad's micro-midget cars.

"Johnny, come down to Planet Earth!" His mom was shaking his shoulder. "Now focus on what I'm saying. We'll be leaving after dark. So be here!"

He sighed, thinking about the ride. They had never been stopped by the police. Still, a dread of what could happen overshadowed even the promise of a new bicycle. If his parents were caught, they might be put in jail. There might be bad things written about them in the newspaper, hurtful things that his friends' parents would read. Then they wouldn't let their children play with him.

And where would they be if Mom and Dad were sent away? They couldn't live alone. He had heard horror stories of orphan- ages and foster homes. It seemed too big a burden to bear even thinking about what could happen. Yet there didn't seem to be any way out. He couldn't tell his father not to take such risks. So he remained quiet, and when the sky turned to shades of black, he and Jean climbed in on the makeshift bed.

The illegal goods were soon safely delivered. Dad went inside to collect his money and have a quick drink with the boys. "Just to be sociable," he said, winking at Mom.

After waiting in the car for about 45 minutes, Mom went inside to see what had happened to Dad. The hours ticked slowly by. At first he and Jean amused themselves by watching men and women going in and out of the party. Most of them went in dressed in suits and ties, but when they came out their shirts were open at the neck and their ties were all crooked. Some were laughing out loud and acting foolish. Some staggered and bumped in to each other. At first it was funny, but after a couple of hours it wasn't funny anymore. It was sickening.

The music floated out the windows and through the doors whenever they opened. It was too dark to play "I spy" or any other games. So they told stories to each other until neither one of them could think of another story. Every time the door opened, they would strain their eyes in the dark, hoping to make out the familiar shapes of their parents. Eventually Jean leaned her head against the window and fell asleep. With nothing else to do, Johnny closed his eyes and dreamed of the shiny blue bike that he hoped to buy soon.

It was after midnight when Mom and Dad stumbled out to the car. At first Dad couldn't find his car keys, and Mom's speech was loud and slurred. Dad accused Mom of losing the keys, and Mom yelled that she hadn't touched the keys. Dad kept telling Mom not to yell so loud. When she didn't listen, he reached over and slapped her. Mom swung back, and the fight was on. By now both kids were wideawake.

"They're stone drunk," Jean whispered to Johnny. "Do you think they can drive?"

They soon found out. Dad almost backed into another car. Mom cursed at him, and then slumped over.

Johnny and Jean moved up to the back of the front seat. About five miles down the road Dad's head began to nod, and the car veered into the left lane. Jean screamed, and Dad jerked the steering wheel. Fortunately there was no traffic so late at night on the roads. The next time Dad began nodding, Johnny stood and leaned over Dad's head and took the wheel.

"Crawl into the front seat," he ordered Jean, "and work the gas pedal and the brakes."

"But how can I?" Jean sobbed in fright.

"Just do it! Get Dad's foot off the gas. You're small enough to sit between him and the steering wheel."

Jean nodded resolutely and obeyed. Johnny knew he could count on her. She was one tough girl. The car squealed to a stop as Jean found the brakes. Then it lurched ahead when she found the gas pedal. She couldn't see that well and depended on Johnny to give concise directions, which he wasn't used to doing. It was a wonder that their heads didn't snap off as the car stopped and started every few feet.

Johnny had his hands full just trying to keep the car in the right lane—steering a car over another person's head isn't easy. Fortunately, both of the kids had experience driving the micro midgets. Somehow their combined efforts got them home. When at last they pulled into the driveway and stopped, Judy came running out to meet them.

"I've been worried sick," she cried. "What happened?"

"We had to drive home," Johnny quietly told her.

Judy looked with disgust at her parents, both of whom were slumped over and out cold. "Well, come on in and get to bed. The sun will be up before long."

"What about Mom and Dad?" Jean asked.

"Leave them there. Serves them right."

Johnny snapped back to the present when the cork on his fishing line disappeared under the water. He pulled the line in, but it was too late. He baited the line again with a fat worm and tossed it back into the water. He'd have to pay more attention.

But not even a hungry fish could keep his thoughts from wandering back to his parents. Alcohol controlled their actions. In its presence they had no thought for anyone but themselves. Dad's driving the previous night could have killed them all. It wasn't fair to put Jean and himself in such danger.

One thing he knew for sure. Alcohol would never be a temptation for him. He knew firsthand how those who drank it became slaves to a stupid bottle. He made up his mind that he would avoid it always.

Chapter 9

Summer was almost at an end. Dried cornstalks dotted the gardens. The tomato vines shriveled in the heat, exposing a few green pieces of fruit clinging beneath the parched leaves. Orange pumpkins brightened the brown fields.

Reluctantly Johnny climbed into the blue station wagon with Judy, Jimmy, Jean, and Mom to go shopping for school clothes. As far as he was concerned shopping was more agonizing than going to the dentist's office. The next-worse thing was sitting in a classroom dissecting sentences when fish could be biting his hook as he sat under a shady tree. Or he could be spinning wheelies on his new shiny blue bicycle.

He and Dale Earnhardt had already made up their minds that neither of them needed to finish school. Both had already learned enough to read street signs and the directions to putting an engine together. What more did a professional race car driver need to know? Practice and determination, they reasoned, could not be found in a book.

One melodious note filled the air. The roar of engines as NASCAR prepared for the biggest races of the year. Eagerly both boys anticipated an eventful season. They saw each other less and less as Dale's father, Ralph, now followed the NASCAR events on a weekly basis. Many of the races were out of state, which didn't bring him to the home track very often. Dale lived in Kannapolis, which was just far enough away to put him in a different school.

When Ralph did visit the racetrack, he often told stories that kept kids sitting on the edge of their seat. There was one in particular that John loved to hear again and again.

Two men drove all day and night to get to the race. When they finally arrived, they fell asleep on the grass, waiting for the chance to compete. They were so tired and were lying so still that no one knew they were there. When it came time for the race to begin, the cars lined up, and one drove right on top of them! They weren't killed, but did wind up speeding to a hospital in an ambulance instead of speeding past the checkered flag.

"Wow!" Johnny exclaimed. "Nothing that exciting ever happens at our track."

"I don't call that exciting," Judy sniffed. "People getting bones crushed is not exciting."

"We can thank the Lord for that," Mom added. "Your dad's accident was all the excitement I can stand."

Somehow the mention of God set Johnny to thinking. Mom had made him attend vacation Bible school at the Methodist church that summer. Many times the teacher had taken him aside to tell him how much God loved him.

"See this picture?" the teacher said, holding up a beautiful scene of two children walking over a perilous bridge. "Their angels are walking right beside them."

"Yes, ma'am," Johnny answered.

"If you love God, your angels will walk beside you, too."

"Do the angels walk beside people who don't love Him?" Johnny asked.

The teacher nodded. "Yes. Angels are there. They can't always keep bad things from happening if we persist in disobeying God, but they are always doing their best to remind us that God loves us."

"I wonder if the angels were beside me driving the car when Dad passed out at the wheel," Johnny muttered under his breath.

"What did you say?" the teacher asked.

"Nothing," Johnny replied.

But the question stayed with him all week. Mom and Dad clearly weren't obeying God. Although he hadn't read much of the Bible that his grandmother had given him, he knew enough to know that alcohol was bad. If it was bad, then it would be disobeying God to drink it. If that was the case, then were his parents bad? Would they not go to heaven because of alcohol? The thought troubled him.

Although he had absolutely no idea where to look, he opened his Bible each night and read a chapter. Some of the words made no sense to him, but others warmed his heart like a tiny puppy snuggled against his chest.

Then something happened at the racetrack that shook Mom and Dad up so much that even they questioned the presence of angels.

The following Sunday the race began like any other. There were foot races for the children and sometimes a micro race in which women competed. Then came the big event. Mom sat behind a small shaded stand next to the radio announcer but close to the track, so she could keep score. All the kids were in the bleachers with Pearly, their closest neighbor, who held Baby Rondy. All the cars lined up as usual. The usual formalities followed. Then they were off.

It wasn't too far into the race when Rondy began crying, and Pearly couldn't quiet him with a pacifier or toys. He wanted to nurse, and he wanted to nurse now. She paced and she bounced him, but he screamed so loud that people began complaining. Finally she sent Judy to get Mom.

Mom got up and hurried away with Judy. She had just reached the bleachers when another car hit James Earnhardt and sent him crashing into the scorekeeper's stand. He hit at such an angle that the roof caved in and boards flew through the air at a deadly speed. The radio announcer scrambled to safety, but the impact was so strong it knocked his pants off. Ordinarily that might have been comical, but everybody knew where Mom was supposed to be. Women began screaming, and men began running to the heap, expecting to pull out her mangled body. But she wasn't there. One man even looked up in the air.

All the while, Baby Rondy cooed and laughed to see his mama.

Did an angel pinch the baby? That night Johnny read his Bible again. This time he looked in the concordance under "angels."

■ ■ ■

Fall passed quickly, and soon winter blew its angry, cold

breath. Snow covered the ground so deeply that all traffic temporarily halted. Even NASCAR called for a shutdown until warmer weather. No teachers tapped for order on their desks. Instead, mothers and fathers paced in front of the windows, praying for the sun to come out and melt that dreadful stuff so the cabin-fevered kids could go back to school.

"Johnny, I've made myself very clear," Mom said for the tenth time that morning. "It's too cold, and you've still got a touch of that flu. Stay inside!"

Johnny's eyes narrowed. Sometimes Mom treated him as though he were a little kid. Sure, he had had the flu. He'd thrown up until his face turned green. But that was yesterday, and now the whole gang was headed for Greer's Pond to ice-skate. "You know it doesn't snow that often here in the South," he argued.

Mom ignored his comment. "Try to get some rest now," she said. "I've got tons of paperwork. If you need something, call Jean or Judy. I don't want to be bothered."

He could hear her footsteps plodding down the hallway. Then the door shut behind her. He could hear the squeak of the chair as she slid it out from the desk. The chair squeaked again as she sat down and scooted it closer to the desk. He could hear her shuffling papers.

Quietly he threw the covers back and tiptoed to his closet. It was so cold out he decided he'd just leave his pajamas on under his jeans.

Jimmy poked his head in the door. "Are you coming?"

"Yes."

"It's your funeral."

The boys slipped to the kitchen where Jean banged some pots and pans for a few minutes so they could shut the door without Mom hearing them leave. Jean and Judy followed a few minutes later.

"You're going to be in sooo much trouble!" Judy scolded as she caught up with them. "You could catch pneumonia."

"I'm fine."

"Well, when Mom tells Dad what you've done, just leave my name out of your defense case."

"Yeah, well, who's going to test the ice if I don't come?"

They all looked at each other and shook their heads. None of them had the nerve to test the ice. Besides, Johnny weighed the least.

"That's what I thought. You don't want to be blamed, but you want me to come."

Nobody said much as they made their way down the road.

"I heard that you can take that path there by Doby's barn," Jimmy broke the silence. "It's a straight shot to the pond."

"Let's do it," Johnny suggested. "If Mom finds out I'm gone, she'll look first on the road."

"I'm game," Jean agreed.

Within minutes they were walking through some of the thickest woods Johnny had ever seen. The path turned out to be a deer trail that twisted and turned through briars and brambles. One trail ran into another one. Fortunately the sound of other boys yelling at the pond led them to the right place.

Johnny felt pretty important that the gang had waited for him. "I guess I'm the only one here with an ounce of courage," he said as he stepped onto the ice.

"Or the only one here without an ounce of sense," Jean smirked.

"There's not one spot in this whole pond that is over my head," Johnny retorted. "So even if the ice does crack, I'll just get wet. At least I'm not afraid of a little water."

"Well, get on with it then," the boys yelled impatiently.

Johnny skated cautiously, gradually working himself all around the pond. When he got to the middle, he held his thumb up. With a whoop and a yell, the others crowded onto the ice. It felt great. The cold air stung his face and filled his lungs.

They skated for about two hours. Jean and Judy kept reminding him that he needed to get back home before Mom discovered an empty bed. If that happened, he would probably be grounded, but at that point he didn't care. He rarely had a chance to slide so effortlessly over frozen water.

Around noon the warming sun began to create cracks in places, and that's when John lost his balance and crashed through the ice. He laughed with everybody else as they pulled him out, dripping wet up to his waist.

"You've got to go home now," Jean ordered. "Take the shortcut through the woods."

Johnny knew he had to go. Uncontrollable shivers swept all over him.

"Hurry!" she urged him on.

He dashed off through the woods, taking the deer trail. His only thoughts now were of crawling into a hot tub of water and soaking his bones for hours. The water on his pant legs was already forming a hard crust of ice. After a few minutes his feet felt numb and heavy. He trudged for 20 minutes through the briars and brambles until he realized that he should have hit the road 10 minutes before. Obviously he had taken the wrong path. He needed to change directions—but which way? The tall trees seemed to stretch out for miles.

He did an about-face and took off in the opposite direction. That only led him back through another 20 minutes of briars and brambles. By now his head was hurting and his nose was stopped up. *OK,* he reasoned, *I'll go to the left.* Twenty minutes later nothing looked familiar. Johnny felt as if he couldn't move another step. His feet had no feeling.

He shouted, hoping that some of the others could hear him, but no one answered. The only thing he could hear was a dog barking in the distance. "O God, I'm going to freeze to death," he sobbed.

Serves you right, a little voice nagged at him. *Thought you were such hot stuff, didn't you? Where's the brave boy now?*

Overwhelmed with discouragement and fear, Johnny sank down on a log. There had to be a way out of this dilemma. It wouldn't have been such a big deal if he weren't wet. He could have walked for hours and found somebody or something familiar. But every step was so painful, and he felt such a weakness coming over him. The flu. No, he wasn't over the flu. He should have listened.

"OK, now what do you do when you're out of answers?" he moaned to himself.

Then he remembered what the lady at Vacation Bible School had told him about God.

He remembered the picture she showed him of the two children on the bridge with the angel watching over them. He remembered the verses he had read in the Bible.

He felt a warm feeling sweep over him as he closed his eyes. "Lord, I know I don't deserve any help, but I'm sick, cold, and lost. Please, help me out of here."

He stayed put on the log, his thoughts suddenly becoming clear. God was there. He couldn't see Him, but he felt His presence. It was warm and assuring.

If only that dog would stop barking . . .

He needed to think. Perhaps if he focused hard enough, God would help him remember some tidbit of advice his dad had given him. Or maybe he could remember something he'd seen on the National Geographic television show about survival . . .

That irritating bark was enough to drive a person crazy! Why, if he had a dog like that—

Then it hit him. Where there were dogs, there were people. *Follow the sound of the dog!* It all made perfect sense now. Why didn't he think of it before? With renewed energy he set off through the woods, making just enough noise and barking himself to keep the dog howling. The barking led him right beside Doby's barn and the road to home.

Later that afternoon, as he soaked in the hot tub, he thought of the warm, fuzzy feeling that he'd had after praying. God was real! And since Mom had grounded him for three days, he had all weekend to think about Him.

Chapter 10

Eventually the snow melted. Old Man Winter sneaked out the back door of February, and March ushered in mild days. Sunshine warmed the earth, coaxing the tiny crocus out of the muddy ground. It was spring, Johnny's favorite time of the year. Favorite, because he never really liked cold weather. Oh, it had its moments when snow painted the landscape white and school was canceled. But most of the time winter wore a gray coat that left Mom depressed.

When spring arrived, new hope seemed to surge through her veins. She combed the nursery for new flowers to plant. Mom loved flowers. Her pink and white azaleas that crowded against the front of the house were the talk of the town. Yellow and white daffodils lined the pathway to the front door. Heavily scented roses of every color bloomed profusely throughout the yard, as did many other flowers Johnny couldn't name (nor did he care to). Flowers were pretty, but a fellow couldn't have a decent game of tag or football without crunching one. Mom tolerated a broken mirror or muddy carpet better than she tolerated a flattened flower.

But aside from warm weather and pretty flowers, Johnny looked forward to another birthday each spring. Mom always made sure that everyone got something they wanted on their birthday. This year Johnny wanted a .22 rifle to hunt squirrels and rabbits. Mom had promised to take him to the store and let him pick it out himself. The anticipation nearly drove him crazy.

March 7 dawned deliciously warm. Johnny bounded out of bed and dressed in record speed. He found Dad in the kitchen frying eggs. "I'm ready to go to the store," he announced.

His dad grinned at his enthusiasm. "Stores aren't even open yet," he pointed out. "It's barely 7:00 a.m. What's the hurry?"

"It's my birthday!"

"So?"

"So I want my rifle."

Dad shrugged. "Are you responsible enough to own a rifle?"

Johnny rolled his eyes. "Dad, I won't shoot at any living thing other than squirrels, rabbits, and deer."

His dad remained silent as he plopped a plate of fried eggs and white rice on the table and motioned for him to sit and eat. Johnny obeyed and poured himself a glass of orange juice. The two ate in friendly silence. The clock on the wall slowly ticked away the minutes. They had almost finished breakfast when Jean bounded into the kitchen and sat down to eat. Ten minutes later Jimmy appeared, followed by Judy, who busied herself wiping counters and washing dishes.

And so the time ticked away. Mom didn't appear until 8:30.

"I'm ready to go!" he greeted her enthusiastically.

Julia only grunted and poured herself a glass of milk. She looked out the window as she drank slowly, often pausing to take in the morning beauty. "I need to water my flowers first, son," she commented.

Johnny sighed and headed outside to wait. It seemed to him that anticipation must be the hardest thing to live with. Hours later he and his mother finally drove off to pick out the most beautiful gun in all the world. He spent the rest of the day in the woods shooting at every animal or flower that moved. The gun made him feel secure, important, and powerful.

Not long thereafter, a one-armed man began coming around the house when Dad was away on trips. Mom glowed in his presence, it seemed to Johnny.

One August afternoon Johnny rounded the corner of the house and saw his mom and the man standing beside his car, talking and laughing. The man reached over and touched Mom's cheek. He was smiling. Johnny wanted to wipe that man's smile right off his face. In his mind this man was stealing Mom from his dad. And since

Dad wasn't there, it was up to him to take care of the situation.

He crept back around the corner and headed for the back door. Dashing through the house, he grabbed his rifle. He'd been itching to use it on something other than squirrels. This lowlife had no right to break up families; he was scum! Didn't he know that Mom had five kids?

He loaded the gun, opened the bedroom window, cocked it, and took careful aim at the man's head. His index finger felt for the trigger. *Steady now,* he told himself. *Hold it steady.*

"Just do it!" the evil angels must have whispered. "Pull the trigger!"

He had no idea what made him hesitate. Maybe in the back of his head he remembered the promise he had made to his dad that he would not shoot at anything other than squirrels, rabbits, and deer. If only he had had heavenly vision at that moment he could have seen an intense battle between the good angels and the evil ones. Both were battling for his soul. Maybe the nurse's prayer requesting that he see with his heart was being answered even then. As the tears streamed down his cheeks, he watched the man get in his car and drive away.

A few months after that experience Dad announced they were moving to Florida. Was it a futile attempt to save his marriage? Did Dad really think he could make more money building highways? Johnny never knew for sure. All he knew was that his world was crashing down around him. Nothing would ever be the same again.

"I can't believe it!" Johnny shouted. "You're closing the track? We're moving where?"

"Calm down, son," James Earnhardt said quietly. "This is for your own good."

"*My* good! How is jerking me out of school and moving me halfway across the country for *my* good?"

"We are not 'jerking' you out of school," Mom told him. "Your dad and I feel that it would be best to get you kids in another environment. Dad's found a steady job that will pay good money. Business at the grill has slowed down, and so has the track. NASCAR has taken over the Sunday racing business."

"Don't worry," Jean put her arm around his shoulders. "Florida is a great place to live. There's alligators and year-round sunshine."

"Better schools, too," Jimmy added.

Johnny shook his head as he stalked out the front door. "Crazy!" he yelled back. "This is crazy!"

"Johnny, come back here!" his mother commanded.

"Let him go," he heard his father say, "He'll be fine once we get there."

With a heavy heart he wandered down to the vacant racetrack. The stands were empty, but in his mind he could see the wheels spinning, the crowds cheering, the dust swirling. He could smell the popcorn and feel the gentle sun on his shoulders. He could see the places where he and the other boys his age played marbles or spun around on their bikes while waiting for the race to begin.

Maybe they would all forget him. It just wasn't fair. How could he leave all this? Saying goodbye was bad enough, but being the new kid at school would be worse. All new kids were snubbed at school. He wasn't even kind to them himself. Now he would know what it felt like.

It didn't take long for Mom to find renters for the house. At least the folks had promised they wouldn't sell it, that one day they would move back. Maybe by then he would be old enough to re-open the track and compete himself.

Dad tried to lift his spirits by promising to take him to the races on Daytona Beach. "You'll see real racing there, son," he promised. "No doubt Ralph and Dale will show up sometime."

The day came when the last box was packed and the last good-bye said. Grandma and Grandpa Earnhardt came to see them off. The old woman's eyes brimmed with tears. "You be good and read that Bible I gave you," she whispered to Johnny.

Johnny nodded, and then they were off.

It didn't take the family long to get settled into their new home, but it took longer to feel settled when it came to school. Had it not been for Jean and Jimmy, Johnny would have run away. There was just something comforting about knowing someone else there, even if it was your older siblings.

Every day after school he rode his bike around town. There were neat springs to swim in and lots of hard-packed trails for riding. Johnny's real intention was to be where the other boys were so they would notice him.

"Hey, you!" one of them finally yelled. "Wanna ride with us?"

Johnny tried to be cool, so he just shrugged. "Depends on where you're riding."

"Down to the drugstore," the biggest boy answered. "Old man Stubbs is real good about giving us free stuff."

"Really?" Johnny perked up. "What kind of stuff?"

"Water guns, candy—all kinds of stuff."

"Let's go!" Johnny yanked up his handlebars, making his bike stand up on the back wheel.

The four boys pedaled down the back streets, and then cut across to Main. The leader of the pack was a tanned boy named Buddy. He was tall and slender with a wide grin that lit up his face. Johnny immediately liked him.

He followed as, one by one, the boys parked their bikes in the alley beside the brick drugstore. "Just watch us and do what we do," Buddy instructed him.

They casually walked into the store and meandered down the aisles. As they passed the gum, Buddy picked up a pack. "You like the pink kind, John?"

"Yeah, it's good."

Buddy slipped it in Johnny's pocket and winked. "Personally," he whispered, "I like the grape." He picked up a pack and bent down, appearing to tie his shoe. But when he straightened up, the gum was gone. He did the same thing with the water guns. One went in his pocket, and one was stuck in his shoe. Johnny wondered how he managed to walk.

He was too confused to know what to do. If he didn't go along with them, they'd snub him even more at school. If he got caught shoplifting, he'd have to face the police and his parents. He just followed in a daze. After a few minutes they all turned and headed for the door as casually as they had walked in.

Suddenly two strong arms grabbed Johnny and Buddy by the shoulder. "What do you boys think you're doing?" a deep voice demanded.

Johnny stared up at the druggist. He was a tall, thin man with the longest fingers he had ever seen. His big hands easily gripped his and Buddy's shoulders so firmly they could barely move.

"What are you boys doing?" the man repeated sternly.

Johnny gulped and began stammering, but Buddy remained cool. "Nothing, Mr. Stubbs. We're just looking around."

"We both know better than that," the man replied icily. "Don't you boys know that shoplifting is stealing? I couldn't afford to stay in business if I let you come in and take anything you wanted. I would have to raise my prices on everything just to pay for what you take. That makes other people have to pay more."

"What's wrong, Lewis?" a woman from behind the counter asked.

"I caught a gang of shoplifters. Phone the police."

The police! Johnny felt the color draining from his face. What would the police do to them? What would his parents do when they found out?

"Oh, please, sir," Buddy cried out. "My father would kill me."

"You should have thought of that sooner," the druggist replied.

"Please, have mercy!" Johnny suddenly blurted out. "We'll give them back and never steal anything again."

"Mercy," the man repeated softly, as if to himself. "Now, what would you know about mercy?" He gazed earnestly into Johnny's eyes.

"If you will forgive me, I'll not only give them back but promise never to step foot in here again."

"Is that so?"

"I promise."

Mr. Stubbs' hand relaxed on their shoulders. Johnny pulled the gum, and everything he had taken, out of his pockets and handed it to the pharmacist. Reluctantly the others did the same. Buddy handed him a water gun and a small pocketknife that Johnny hadn't even seen before. How in the world had he gotten all that stuff without him seeing it? And he had been right behind him!

"OK, boys," Mr. Stubbs said. "I don't want to see you in this store without your parents. Is that clear?"

The whole group nodded and began bumping into each other in their haste to get out before Mr. Stubbs could change his mind. When they reached the alley Buddy bent over and ceremoniously pulled out a second water gun that had been wedged between his sock and high-top shoe. "That's why you always take two," he gloated.

The others gave him a high five. "Good going, Buddy!" they shouted.

Johnny stood there in disbelief. Mr. Stubbs had been so kind to them. It just didn't seem right. "I gotta go," he finally said as he mounted his bike.

"See you tomorrow," the others called to him as he rode off.

Johnny didn't reply. Those boys were considered cool by most of the kids at school. Yet they boldly lied and stole from a man who had just showed them mercy. Johnny didn't feel good about stealing anything from such a kind man. *But,* he reasoned, *I won't ever steal from him again.* Though neither Johnny nor Mr. Stubbs could know it then, Johnny would one day become Mr. Stubbs's pastor. But that would take some time and a whole lot of work on God's part to help Johnny reach the place where he would be willing to follow Jesus with his whole heart. In the meantime he pushed the still small voice aside and continued to hang out with Buddy and his followers.

■ ■ ■

The years of 1962 to 1964 were big years in the racing world. Men such as Richard Petty, Bobby Isaac, Junior Johnson, and Fireball Roberts were at the height of their career. While racing was mushrooming and ordinary blue-collar workers were suddenly becoming household names, another flame was igniting in Florida. Racial tension had become front-page news.

On a family vacation to St. Augustine, James and Julia accidentally found themselves in the middle of a protest. The Blacks, along with White sympathizers, were marching down to a "Whites only" beach. Up to that point no one but Caucasians had the privilege of choosing any beach they liked.

A fight broke out. Police officers rushed in, and somehow a little boy was killed by an officer. Johnny never understood how it happened. It was even unclear as to who was fighting whom, as Whites were fighting both Blacks and Whites, and vice versa. The city of St. Augustine had become a battlefield. Johnny watched as his mother jumped right in the middle of the crowd and grabbed another White woman by her hair. The two were tumbling on the ground and slamming their fists into each other.

A gunshot rang out.

Without taking his eyes from the scene, Johnny reached out to hold his little brother's hand. His other siblings had gone off in another direction earlier in the day, and now with both parents suddenly gone, it was up to him to shield Rondy. But no little hand clutched his in response. He spun around frantically, searching the sea of confusion for a little blond-haired boy. He called his name and started running away from the crowd. Had someone stolen his brother, or had he run for safety?

Ten minutes passed, and still no Rondy. Johnny plunged into the crowd and found his mother. "Rondy is gone!" he shouted. "I can't find him anywhere!"

Alarm spread over Julia's face. Somehow she found James and the others and began a detailed search through the city. They finally found the little tyke huddled in a clump of bushes in the park, next to the former slave market.

Those were turbulent years as the nation once again was divided against itself over the issue of basic human rights.

That same year Fireball Roberts was severely burned when his car spun backward on the seventh lap into a concrete wall and immediately exploded into flames. He died about a month later from burns, pneumonia, and blood poisoning.

On September 22, 1964, Jimmy Pardue, who had competed against James in micro-midgets at the beginning of his racing career, was testing tires at the same track in Charlotte, North Carolina. On the seventh lap a tire exploded, throwing his car through the guardrail. Splintered wood slashed through the air. The car flipped and landed in a dried-up creek. Jimmy died two and a half hours later at the Cabarrus Memorial Hospital in Concord.

James had followed the career of these two men, and now they were gone. Although he said little, he mourned their passing. He had often wondered if he had done the right thing in getting out of racing. At this moment, it seemed so. He continued working on Interstate 4 in Florida, and the family moved several times to follow the trail of asphalt. But when the job was finished, he was ready to move back to North Carolina.

Johnny had kept track of Ralph Earnhardt and his son, Dale. Both boys had changed so much. Johnny came back to North Carolina driving a red motorcycle, even though he was only 15 years old. (At that time the state of Florida allowed a teen to get a driver's license at the age of 14.) But once he arrived in North Carolina, a state trooper pulled him over and forced him to park it.

Since he couldn't drive it on a state highway, Johnny would

often go down to the decaying racetrack and spin around the curves. Sometimes he would stop and think about all the fun he and his friends had had while watching the cars zoom past the checkered flag. He and Dale had been two boys with big dreams of one day living a life of speed and glory. Somehow the dream had lost its intensity for him. He knew his life would take a different direction, but he didn't know where.

James now scoffed at the idea of reopening the track. Micro-midget racing was not big enough to compete with NASCAR. Racing was slowly becoming a full-time sport and was no longer a part-time pleasure.

Dale, though, had remained steadfast in his quest to be with his dad on the track. He thought of little else but racing. He was not happy going to school. He and his dad fought over it constantly.

"It was the only thing I ever let my daddy down over," Dale would say in 1987. "He wanted me to finish. It was the only thing he ever pleaded with me to do. But I was so hardheaded. For about a year and a half after that we didn't have a close relationship."

Nevertheless, Ralph Earnhardt was a master mechanic and began teaching Dale how to build engines. Sometimes he would give Dale used tires and various car parts to tinker with. As soon as he received his license, Dale began speeding through life in the fast lane, driving whatever vehicle he could scrape up the money for. Although Dale was just a beginner, he finished in the top six of a Sportsman race, thereby earning him the right to compete in the Grand National against his own father.

Of course, Dale didn't have the experience or the engine the other Grand National racers had. One driver simply would not let him go by. Dale did everything he knew to pass, but couldn't. So his father, who was already a lap ahead, came up from behind and put his bumper against Dale's. He pushed him right by the other guy, enabling Dale to win third place.

In many ways our Father in heaven is like that. We cannot defeat the devil in our own power. But if we give the steering wheel of our life over to Him and ask Him to do what we can't, He will steer us through the bad times and across the finish line. And while this Bible verse doesn't pertain to a sport like NASCAR, it does apply to each of us. "He shall feed his flock like a shepherd: he shall gather the lambs with his arm, and *carry them* in his bosom" (Isaiah 40:11).

Chapter 12

1966. John cradled the driver's license in his hand. Now he could drive in whichever state he chose. He stared at his picture. Mom said he should have smiled bigger, but that would have looked as if he was overeager. Nah! Only nerds smiled real big for their driver's license.

"Let me see it," his dad asked as he leaned over the chair where John sat in the sunny kitchen. John handed him the small card. His father held it out from his face in an effort to see better. "H'mmm, I can't see your eyes."

"Daaaad!" John reached for the license. "You need glasses."

James turned slightly, holding John at bay. "Really. I can't see your eyes! How can they use this picture to identify you? Boy, you need a haircut. Are you that broke? What does a cut cost now, $5?"

John groaned. Not again! Why did everybody have to make such a deal over the length of his hair? He heard it in every class at school. He heard it when he walked by the principal standing in the hall. Wasn't he studying the price Americans paid to have freedom? In the old days men wore wigs of long hair. Even George Washington, the first president of the United States, wore a long braid down his back. What was the big deal over a little hair touching your eyebrows or your ears? He winced. Perhaps changing the subject would get Dad talking about something else.

"Dad, I want to go look at cars this week."

"You got any money?"

"Some."

"How much is some?"

John shrugged. "A couple hundred."

It was James's turn to sigh. "I've got a load to deliver tomorrow. How about Friday?"

John perked up. "You mean it?"

"Yeah. We'll look. Are you sure you can see to drive?"

It was past 7:00 on Friday evening when James walked in the door, tired, hungry, and dirty. John wasn't in the mood to hear his excuses. Hadn't his dad made a promise? Why, he wondered, were parents so irresponsible? Especially when it came to things that were important to their children. He had been pacing the floor since 4:00 in the afternoon.

James said little as John ranted and raved over his lateness. A wreck on the interstate had kept traffic at a standstill for more than an hour. Then the load he was supposed to pick up wasn't ready. But he knew that nothing he said would change things, so he grabbed a pack of cookies out of the cupboard, took a cold soda from the fridge, and silently walked out the door.

John followed, wondering if his father would actually go through with his promise. James climbed into the red pickup truck, and John quickly did the same. He settled back on the blackened seat that smelled of grease and cigarette smoke. One day he wouldn't have to depend on Dad or Mom to drive him to town. He could see himself now, cruising down Main Street, with the windows open and his radio blaring. Of course, it wouldn't be a new car. No dealer sells new cars for a couple of hundred. But it would be new to him.

"What kind of car are you looking for?"

John braced himself for his dad's reaction. "I'd like a 1955 Chevy."

"I can't believe you!" his father sputtered. "We've always had Fords in this family. Why would you want a Chevy?"

"I like 'em.

"Are you trying to make me the laughingstock of the family? I can just hear Ralph and Dale going on about that."

"They'd drive anything that ran."

James shook his head. Where had he gone wrong with this boy? He never did things the way he had been taught. Ralph raced in a Ford all the time—and won!

They drove the rest of the way to the used-car lot in silence. Neither said much as they surveyed the lot. His dad stopped to admire a black Ford Starliner. Next to that was a 1964 Ford Falcon. John briefly noticed the sky-blue color, the chrome wheels, and the modified engine with a stick shift in the floor.

Then he saw it—a 1955 Chevy sitting in the corner like a lovely pearl in the midst of sewage. It was love at first sight. He raced over and gingerly touched the dark metallic blue hood. Gently lifting it, he gaped at the souped-up 283 engine. Closing the hood carefully, he walked around the body, taking in the mag wheels and the dent-free sides. The doors were locked, but he could see the four-speed stick shift on the floor. This was it—*the car of his dreams!*

James Earnhardt meandered over and shook his head. "How much is it?"

John tore his gaze from the roll-pleated interior. "What?"

"How much does it cost? You're standing in front of the price sheet."

John glanced down. "Only $300."

"You have only $200, son," James reminded him.

John's face fell. "Can't you help me out? I'll pay you back."

"The lot is closed, son. We need to talk about this anyway. We'll come back Monday."

"It may be sold by Monday."

"I doubt it. Now come on. I'm starved."

The ride home wasn't as silent as the ride over had been. John raved about the wonderful car. He pointed out that the vehicle hadn't been wrecked, as far as he could tell. The color was his favorite, and he would work hard till the day he died to pay for it.

James said little. If only it was a Ford. He wouldn't mind contributing for a Ford. But a *Chevy?* In all his life he never knew one Earnhardt who drove a Chevy.

But like all fathers who love their sons, James eventually compromised his staunch convictions about Chevys, and John triumphantly drove the car home on Monday evening.

The car did little to increase John's attentiveness at school. He stayed out late each night with his friends and dozed during class the next day. He sped through town on his first date in the blue Chevy, now lovingly called "Betsy," and received his first ticket. His teachers tried to impress him with the importance of an education, but like Dale, John had already made up his mind that education was a pain in the neck.

John was dismissed from school in the ninth grade for smoking in the bathroom. Julia stormed into the office and closed the door. John never heard what she said, but he was allowed to come back the next day. By the tenth grade his record was so reprehensible that she couldn't even bribe the principal into allowing him to come back.

By then Judy and Jimmy were in college, studying to be teachers. Then Jean got married, and that left only John and Rondy at home. With most of his siblings gone, the word "home" didn't conjure up pleasant memories anymore. Dad must have felt the same way. He bought an 18-wheeler and took long trips that left Mom alone with her friend, the bottle. When he did come home, Mom suspected infidelity, and their harsh words frequently resulted in bloody fistfights.

Their fighting kept him in constant fear that one would eventually kill the other, as they had almost done when he was 10. That quarrel made such an impression on his mind that he would forever remember the details. Every time they argued he dredged up the memories of that day so long ago.

John had been inside the house, playing with Jean and Rondy. Loud, angry voices from the tavern caused the children to walk out on the back porch to listen. They could hear their parents swearing and yelling at each other. Suddenly a loud penetrating shout made him instinctively bolt from the porch and through the back door of the tavern. He found his dad standing in the middle of the floor, bleeding profusely from a cut on his head. The look in his eyes was a mixture of pain and disbelief. Mom stood in front of him, holding a ketchup bottle. Her eyes were defiant and blazing.

"Get out of here, Johnny," she yelled. "This is between your daddy and me."

John backed into the kitchen area and grabbed a few towels.

He doused one in cold water, handed them to his father, and ran.

Later his mother approached him with a school album. She turned the pages until she found the picture of a young girl that his best friend liked. "Do you see this girl, Johnny?"

"Yes, Mom," he answered. "What about her?"

"You are never to date or marry this girl."

He looked at her with wide eyes. He was too young even to think about marriage. "Why, Mom?"

"She's your half sister." She practically spit the words out and stalked out of the room.

John could not understand his parents' relationship. If one of them got sick, the other went out of their way to care for the sick one. Mom's bad back sent her to the hospital for an operation. When she returned home and was confined to bed, Dad would get the mail and lay it on her bed each morning. He would stop at a restaurant and buy her food and bring it to her. But when she was better, the battles resumed.

It was as though they loved and despised each other at the same time. It would not be that way with him, John vowed. Yet, while he hated his parent's lifestyle, he found himself doing some of the same things he had so despised in them. Like his father, he smoked two packs of cigarettes daily and guzzled beer on the weekends. Cigarettes and beer gave him a cool image to his peers. For some stupid reason that he couldn't even fathom, he needed that image.

But inside he felt as though he was spiraling downward in a dark hole with no light at the bottom. To top it off, his girlfriend of two years had dumped him.

It was in January that fate stepped in at a high school basketball game. Nothing would be the same again.

During intermission he saw a young girl standing in the hallway, talking with some other girls. Her long auburn hair immediately caught his attention—it wasn't red, and it wasn't brown. It was sort of the color of an Irish setter, and it almost touched her waist. She laughed a lot. He stood and watched her for a few minutes. He knew he had to meet her.

His buddy, David Eagle, jabbed him in the arm. "Go for it," he winked.

John combed his long hair and cleared his throat. Had he been that obvious? But he couldn't back away, not with David watching. That wouldn't be cool. But what if she snubbed him?

When he finally got the nerve to walk over to her, she looked up with such smiling green eyes that he forgot all formalities. "What's your name, baby?" he blurted out.

And that was my formal introduction to John Earnhardt.

Shocked, I averted my eyes. What a cocky jerk! I looked over at my friends, hoping for a little support. They giggled and walked away. That left the two of us standing alone, both feeling terribly awkward. Not knowing what else to do, I answered, "My name is Crystal."

"Crystal?"

"Bringle," I added.

Then it hit him. I was the little sister of one of his friends! He looked around, half expecting to see my brother coming toward him with a switchblade. By now the intermission was over, and we were practically alone in the hallway.

I had a habit of laughing when I was nervous, which made him think that I was delighted by his wit. He took that as a good sign and started cracking jokes and talking. I relaxed, and by the end of the evening he had taken me to the parking lot to show off his Chevy. He had spent every available weekend and a few hours each evening pumping gas to pay his dad back.

"It's nice," I said, running my hands over the metallic blue paint. "I love this color."

"You do?"

"Of course. It matches your eyes. Have you given it a name?"

He nodded. "I call her Betsy."

I raised my eyebrows. "You named her after a *girlfriend?*"

"No. It just seemed to fit the car."

I smiled, and he took my hand and lifted it toward the light. "Do you ever get out in the sun?"

I frowned. "Yes! I'm just cursed with fair skin."

He looked at my face. There wasn't a zit on it. Just a few freckles sprayed over a small nose that tilted up slightly on the end. "I don't really think that's a curse. You're beautiful."

Instantly my white cheeks turned into a blushing pink. I pulled my hand back. "We'd better get inside before the game ends. My brother will be looking for me."

Later that night he lay in bed smoking a cigarette and watching the brown plaid curtains flutter at the window. He could hear his parents in the next room getting louder and louder. The insults and bursts of anger drafted through the thin bedroom walls. Must his parents begin and end every weekend with an argument? Would they never be happy?

He took his pocket calendar out of his wallet and circled the date. It had been a special night. Maybe something would come of it.

rom that special night in January until the end of school, John and I met at every basketball game and sat together. We were too young for a serious relationship, but somehow neither of us could stop the magnetic pull that drew us together. By the time summer arrived, John couldn't stand the thought of me even talking to another boy. The fact that I attended another school and couldn't be with him every day bothered him. In his eyes I was his girl. Surely every boy must be vying for my attention, and he wasn't there to protect me from the other boys who might look my way. Was I being true to him?

In his limited exposure to women, he knew one thing to be sure: they couldn't be trusted. He remembered his mom and the one-armed man. While one battle may have been won that day, another was lost. Since that time John had no trust in the female population. If your own mother would betray her family, what would a girlfriend do for a little attention?

For my part, I resented being questioned about every conversation I had at school. John could be so much fun; he could be so easy to talk to. Why did he have to ruin a good thing by interrogating me every day? I couldn't even go shoe shopping with my mom without having to describe what the salesman looked like and what he said to me. Our relationship bounced up and down so much that by mutual agreement we agreed to break up by July. He knew we were in way over our heads.

In order to forget me, John tried to join the Coast Guard but was turned down. In desperation he asked his cousin, Tony, to go with him to Florida. Maybe a change of scenery would do him good. He needed to see some of the old gang. Maybe date a few of his old girlfriends. The two left in high spirits. A couple weeks later they were back. It didn't take him long to find the phone. He couldn't forget me.

■ ■ ■

Although John and Dale had no contact during their teen years, the way their lives went one might have thought that they kept a day-by-day account of what the other was doing and decided to imitate each other. Both dropped out of school the same year. Dale went to work at Cannon Mills during the day, and John worked there at night. Dale married when he was 17, and so did John. (However, Dale divorced at age 19.)

The marriage ceremony for John and me took place in the local Lions Club building. I wore a pale-yellow dress, covered in white lace, that belonged to my sister, and borrowed Jean's white veil. John put on a suit and cut his hair, much to my disgust. "Your hair has never been that short," I whispered to him as we stood in front of the minister. "It seems as though I'm marrying a stranger."

"My mom made me," he whispered back. "But don't worry; it'll grow back. With our budget we won't be able to afford haircuts anyway."

After the ceremony we drove to Myrtle Beach for the weekend. The car overheated every 20 minutes, and we had to stop to add water. I had been to the beach only once and didn't realize how easy it was to get sunburned. I soon turned beet red and was so sore John could barely hug me.

The following months were a blur of ups and downs. Young love is usually 80 percent physical and 20 percent personality. When you're young you feel that you can change anyone. Twenty against 80 doesn't seem that bad when the other party just promised to climb the highest mountain or swim the deepest river for you. Of course, that promise didn't include getting up when you're tired just to fix a drink for the other person, or keeping your mouth shut when the meal tasted awful and you were really hungry. Swimming a river has nothing to do with saying kind things when there isn't a kind thought in your head. But the popular song of that day warbled something about following him wherever he may go. There wasn't an ocean too deep or a mountain too high to climb to keep the singer away from following her love.

I was too young and immature to handle the responsibilities of being married, and in spite of John's determination to not be like his parents, he mirrored their attitudes. He used the precious little money he earned to buy cigarettes and beer. We couldn't afford our own apartment and were forced to move in with his parents. I was pregnant now, and he hated to expose me to his parents' fights and drinking binges, but he didn't have any options.

Just when things couldn't get any worse, the Lord used a tragic accident to turn our lives in a new direction. One day Ruth Oliver had a thought, no doubt suggested to her by the Holy Spirit to help answer her own long-ago prayer that she had whispered in the bootleggers' shanty 19 years before.

Chapter 14

One evening John and I walked in the door to find Julia sitting by the phone, sobbing hysterically. "She's dead!" she moaned, swaying back and forth on the couch. "My sister is dead!"

Eventually we were able to get her into bed and call John's dad. He paced around the room, stopping sometimes to awkwardly pat her on the shoulder. John made a few phone calls and pieced the story together. An oncoming vehicle had swerved into Aunt Pearl's lane as she rounded a curve. The crash killed her instantly.

Julia spent the next few days taking tranquilizers and visiting relatives.

"Her drinking is going to get worse after this," John worried aloud. "Aunt Pearl and Mom were close."

That evening a strange woman knocked on the door. "My name is Grace Robbins," she introduced herself. She was tall with short silvery hair and large blue eyes. "Dr. and Mrs. Oliver asked me to come over."

"Dr. Oliver?" Julia exclaimed. "Why would he do that?"

"Well, actually it was Mrs. Oliver—Ruth. You are a patient of theirs, aren't you?"

"Yes, but I don't understand."

"They belong to my church," Grace explained. "They heard that you just lost your sister." She smiled warmly and held Julia's hand. "I just wanted to tell you how sorry our church is about your loss. The Bible has some very precious promises to comfort us during times like this. May I share a few of them with you and then pray?"

"I would appreciate any comfort you can offer." Julia stepped back and motioned for her to sit down. "I've been close to losing my mind with grief."

After a round of introductions to the whole family, Grace asked, "Does everyone have a Bible? I would like for each one of you to see these wonderful promises for yourself."

John nodded and found three dusty Bibles. One of them was from his grandmother, and another was from attending Vacation Bible School when he was a child.

Grace helped them find the book of First Thessalonians in the New Testament. Then she asked them to take turns reading the verses. Together they read chapter 4, verses 16-18:

"'For the Lord himself shall descend from heaven with a shout, with the voice of the archangel, and with the trump of God: and the dead in Christ shall rise first: then we which are alive and remain shall be caught up together with them in the clouds, to meet the Lord in the air: and so shall we ever be with the Lord. Wherefore comfort one another with these words.'"

"Jesus is coming again," Grace told them. "He said, 'I am the resurrection, and the life: he that believeth in me, though he were dead, yet shall he live.' If your sister believed in Jesus with all of her heart, she will live again at the resurrection." Grace then explained how death was like a sleep, a rest from life's labors. They read from the book of Revelation about Jesus coming as a triumphant king, welcomed by some, dreaded by others.

The whole family drank in the words, but I was especially interested in studying the Bible.

"I can sense that each one of you would like to learn more about God's Holy Word," Grace concluded. "I have a series of studies that I think you will enjoy." She reached into her bag and pulled out a little blue booklet with the words *The Bible Says* printed on the cover. "This is real easy to do," she explained. "I can leave one lesson with each of you now to read and to look up the Bible texts. I'll stop by next week and see if you have any questions. Then I'll give you lesson two. I even have a free King James Bible that has the pages correlated with the questions."

John shook his head. "I don't have time for that kind of stuff, but Crystal and Mom might enjoy it."

To his surprise, Julia Earnhardt nodded in approval.

■ ■ ■

During the next few months John noticed a change in me. I faithfully studied my Bible every day and answered the questions in *The Bible Says* lessons. In the evenings, when he came home from work, I'd be sitting on the bed, waiting to share with him what I'd read.

"Did you know that the Ten Commandments are an expression of God's character?" I asked him one night. "He died because of a broken law. The penalty for a broken law is death, but Jesus decided to take the punishment for us. He allowed wicked men to crucify Him. It was humanity who had broken the law, but He took our punishment."

John stood in shock, not knowing what to say. Was this the same girl he married?

"The only thing that He asks in return," I continued, "is that we love Him enough to obey Him. He says, 'If ye love me, keep my commandments' [John 14:15]." I then proceeded to read the commandments out loud to him.

John continued to stare at me. He thought I was getting into this Bible stuff too deep. "You're not becoming a Holy Roller, are you? I've heard of people who've lost their minds over religion."

I turned away from him, my voice quivering a little. "I feel like I need something more in my life. I just thought the Bible could provide a measure of happiness." I fell silent for a moment and cleared my throat, trying to gain control. Then I turned toward him with determination. "It wouldn't hurt you, either, you know."

He could sense the sadness in my voice. Did I really expect him to get all weepy-eyed over the Bible, or to turn into some clean-shaven, Bible-thumping hysteric? Hadn't he tried reading it once before?

"I am perfectly happy," he told me, trying to sound as light-hearted as he could. He sat down on the bed and pulled me against his chest. "With a beautiful wife like you, how could I be otherwise?"

"You have been in the sun too long," I said, pulling away from him. "My hair is a mess, my clothes are too tight, and I smell like Lysol and dirty mop water. Your mom wanted the kitchen floor cleaned today."

"And dutiful, too!" he teased. "What more could a guy ask for?" He gave me a long and lingering kiss. But in his heart he knew happiness was deeper than a pretty wife and a clean kitchen.

Chapter 15

*M*onths before, when he first found out that I was expecting a baby, John went to his father, who sat at the kitchen table logging the deliveries he had made with his 18-wheeler. "Dad," he said, "I've got something serious to talk with you about."

James Earnhardt looked up from the mound of papers in front of him. "Go ahead; I'm listening."

John got right to the point. "I'm going to be a father. Crystal is pregnant."

James's face remained almost expressionless. "If I were you, son," he said dryly, "I'd take the first flight to Cuba." He wrote a few numbers down on his paper, then added, "Kids don't stay cute very long. If you don't believe me, just look in the mirror." He looked back down at his papers, his very actions telling John that that was all he had to say on the subject.

Disgusted, John walked through the woods to the old racetrack. For some reason it was just the best place to be when a fellow needed to sort things out. At first he was angry with his father. Couldn't he show some sort of emotion? Would it kill him to give some thoughtful advice? This child would be his grandchild. Didn't that mean anything to him? John knew that he himself had come into this world uninvited. His dad was probably no more excited when Julia told him that she was expecting his child than he was now about a grandchild.

Yet his father had stayed. He remembered him getting up and cooking breakfast for all the kids. He remembered the beginnings of the racetrack, and how much fun the whole family had had. Maybe Dad had given up the racetrack to give them a better lifestyle, a better heritage. It would have been nice to hear him say something to indicate that, but Dad just didn't talk for the sake of talking. He almost acted as if he didn't know how.

Somehow seeing the racetrack had given him a warmer picture of his father. It made him decide to do the right thing. He would be a good father, but he would talk to his children more. He left the racetrack feeling much better.

And now with me studying the Bible so much, he felt a need to go back to the racetrack and sort things out again. He walked down the road that was now overgrown with weeds and potholes. Small bushes and trees cluttered the once cleared land. The bleachers were broken and sagging. The field was quiet. No cheering except for the birds that seemed to be happy with the calm. There was horse manure on the track. He knew some of the neighbors used the track to ride their horses.

He sat for hours, replaying in his mind the things that had happened there. The day his father was flipped and his car burst in flames. He remembered the fear as they tried to cut him out of the seat belt. God was there then.

Then he saw another car tearing through the scorekeeper's stand where his mother had been just minutes before. Another footprint of God.

He had preserved their lives so many times. At one time he had felt so close to God. He had prayed for God to lead him, had prayed for his parents to quit drinking. Why hadn't God answered his prayers?

He lit a cigarette and inhaled deeply. One of the points that Grace Robbins always emphasized was the importance of loving Jesus enough to obey Him. "Our God is a loving Father," she had said over and over. "Everything He asks you to do is for your own good. The Ten Commandments are perfect. If we would obey them, we would be perfectly happy. They are not, as some people think, a burden or optional."

"But I understood that they were done away with at the cross," he remembered his mother objecting. "The apostle Paul taught that."

"Let's turn to 1 Corinthians 6:10," Grace answered. She then read, "'Nor thieves, nor covetous, not drunkards, nor revilers, nor extortioners, shall inherit the kingdom of God.'"

"If the commandments are done away with, then why would it be wrong to be covetous or be a thief? Verse 11 condemns adultery. How could such acts be breaking the law if there is no such law in effect? God isn't wishy-washy, changing His mind so that it's unclear to His children what is expected of them. In reality, what God really wants is for us to be like Him—good and pure. Fortunately, He spelled it out with His own finger in stone."

"I always did wonder why He wrote them in stone," I said. "You can't erase something written in stone."

"No, you can't." Grace replied. "But you must understand that we can't keep this law by ourselves. It is only when we invite Jesus to live in our hearts that we can live like Jesus. Only, it's Jesus living through us giving us strength and wisdom. That's found in Philippians 2:13 and 4:13."

John tossed the cigarette down and crushed it with his foot. That was a new thought. God living in John Earnhardt. If only it could be that easy. He could hear me calling for him. He turned around and took one last look at the track he loved so dearly and headed back through the woods toward home.

■ ■ ■

The lazy days of autumn vanished, replaced by biting winds and icy rains. Days became shorter, bringing in the dark by 6:00.

"I need a few things at the store," Julia told her son one evening. "The weather forecast is calling for snow tomorrow. Would you run into town for me?"

"Sure." He looked at me, now round as an overgrown pumpkin. "Want to go along?"

"I will do anything to get out of this house," I muttered as I tried to rock myself off the couch. John reached out a hand and pulled me up on the third try.

The nearest grocery store was out of fresh garlic, and Julia had said not to come back without it. She planned to make a pot of spaghetti sauce tomorrow morning and let it simmer all day. So in spite of the slippery road conditions, we decided to try another grocery store about 10 miles away. It didn't take long to purchase the needed items and put them into the trunk of John's old Chevy.

I was hugging myself for warmth while waiting for John to unlock the doors. Suddenly a sharp pain made me cry out and grab my stomach.

"Are you OK?" John's face turned white as he helped me into the cold car. "Let me get the heater running. It's not time for the baby yet, is it?"

"No." Tears of fright threatened to spill over at any moment. I was completely stressed out. He better get me home right away.

He put the key in and turned the ignition switch. Nothing happened. "Not now," he groaned. "Come on, Betsy, start." Still nothing. In spite of the cold, sweat trickled down his face. Jumping out of the car, he lifted the hood. After a few minor adjustments, he tried again, but to no avail. "Not now!" He slammed his fist into the steering wheel and let out a string of profanity.

"John, let's pray," I suggested.

"Crystal, I'm not in the mood for a sermon." He ran his fingers through his hair and glared at me. "Don't you see how icy the roads are becoming? I'd better go for help. Are you all right? Any more pains?"

I tuned him out. "'Trust ye in the Lord for ever: for in the Lord Jehovah is everlasting strength,'" I whispered. "Isaiah wrote that." I turned to him, and there was no fright at all in my face anymore. "This isn't a sermon, John; it's important that I know."

"Know what?" he demanded. *Is she going out of her head or what?*

"God wants to prove to us that He is real, that we can trust Him with our lives. John, can you start the car?"

"No, Crystal, I can't! What do you think I've been trying to do?"

"Will you try one more time?"

Without answering, he leaped out of the car and jerked the hood up. I think he was glad that I couldn't see the mixture of fright and anger on his face. The roads were icy, his car wouldn't start, and his wife was going loony. Or maybe women did that when they went into labor!

A few cars slid around on the slick pavement as people hurried home. No one bothered to ask if we needed help. A few minutes later he slammed the hood shut and rubbed his hands furiously as he made his way to the car. He twisted the key.

Silence.

"That's good, John." I couldn't hide the excitement in my voice. "We know that you can't start the car. Now, let's pray and ask God to make it run."

"Crystal!"

"Please, John."

Nodding, he bowed his head. What else could he do?

"Dear Lord," I began, "You know we need to get home where it's warm. You know that the roads are icy and dangerous. Please do what we can't do. Please start the car. Thank You, Lord. In Jesus' name. Amen."

He reached once more for the ignition.

"Wait a minute." I stopped his hand from touching the key. "Give Him a chance to work."

John sighed but said nothing. It would be quicker than arguing with me.

After a minute or two I nodded, and John turned the key. The gentle purr of the old Chevy engine sounded like music from heaven. He looked at me, surprise written all over his face. Had God really been there all along, waiting and hoping that He would get the chance to answer his doubts and nourish a seed of faith in his heart?

I smiled and leaned back in the seat. "Let's go home, John."

Chapter 16

John grunted under the heavy weight of the caskets he was loading onto the truck. Methodically he lifted and pushed, lifted and pushed, while his foreman barked commands like an Army drill sergeant. He knew he should be concentrating on getting the shipment out, but his thoughts kept drifting homeward. Was Crystal all right? The baby could come any time now, according to the doctor. Would he soon have a son, or would it be a delicate little girl? Would Crystal make it? *What would I do if something happened to her?* he asked himself. She's so young.

"What's wrong, Earnhardt?" the foreman yelled. "Did you forget to eat your Cheerios this morning? Moving kind of slow, aren't you?" He laughed out loud, rude and coarse. "Come on; step on it!"

As John quickened his pace he thought how at such times he wanted to take his job and shove it in old Brickett's face. But then how would he pay for the hospital and doctor bill? Suddenly he thought of his friends at school. He could be sitting in English class right now, snoring away with them, instead of breaking his back. He remembered how the principal had once warned him that those who didn't get an education would be pumping gas into their former classmates' expensive cars. "You should be nice to the nerds who study," he had said. "They'll be your boss one day."

Well, he wasn't working for one of them yet, but it certainly would be easier than making boxes to bury people in. At least it wouldn't give you calluses.

The noon whistle blew. All the men dropped their loads instantly. No one wanted to waste one second of lunch break. Some headed for their trucks, while others gathered in clusters to rest and eat. John grabbed his lunch box and joined a small group by the loading box. Most of them were cracking jokes about sex and women.

"Hey, I know this place where we can have some fun tonight!" one exclaimed. "We could drink a few cold beers and shoot pool. Who wants to go?"

Most of the men roared their approval.

"What about you, son?"

John looked up to find the whole group staring at him. "Are you too wet behind the ears to enjoy a man's game?"

Rather pleased that they had noticed him, John smiled. "I'm with you."

The older man laughed and slapped his knee. "Good. Maybe we can teach you a few facts of life."

John couldn't help thinking that he had learned the facts of life the hard way. There was nothing they could add that he didn't already know. He wondered what he'd find when he eventually did get home. He knew I'd be angry, but didn't he have a right to enjoy life occasionally without me? For all he knew, I could be planning on ditching him as soon as the doctor bills were paid.

That evening he tried to smother his nagging conscience. The men beat him in a few games of pool and won 10 of his hard-earned dollars. After a few beers, John excused himself, declaring that he had to go straighten his wife out.

On the way home he tried to brace himself for the cold shoulder treatment that I could so effectively dish out. Well, what did it matter? So he had had some fun. It was his body, his money. He could do what he wanted.

I was propped up on the bed with the black Book in my hands when he walked into the bedroom. A smile spread across my face. "Oh, John! I'm so glad you're home. I've just read the most beautiful Bible verses. Would you like to hear them?"

At first he was too stunned to answer. It wasn't the kind of greeting he'd anticipated, but if I wanted to play games, he would cruise along.

"OK, dish it out."

"This is found in 1 Corinthians 6:19, 20: 'What? know ye not that your body is the temple of the Holy Ghost which is in you, which ye have of God, and ye are not your own? For ye are bought with a price: therefore glorify God in your body, and in your spirit, which are God's.'"

"I don't get it." He didn't dare sit down—he might need a fast exit. So he stood there and stared at me.

"You know how people are always saying that it's their body and they can do what they want with it?"

Oh, no! he thought. *She can read my mind.*

"Well," I continued, oblivious to his thoughts, "that's not true. I've been reading the lesson Grace dropped off this morning. It says that Christ paid for our bodies with His blood. That's how much He loves you and me. Our bodies don't belong to us anymore. They are supposed to be the dwelling place for the Holy Spirit. For you are 'bought with a price,' the Bible says; 'therefore glorify God in your body.'"

Understanding dawned in his mind gradually, like the morning sun gliding over the hills and valleys. He stood there while the Holy Spirit knocked at the door of his heart. "I love you, John," it seemed to say. "I will never leave you nor forsake you. Everybody else may abandon you, but I am solid like a rock. I won't bend with the winds of change. I am everlasting and eternal. I have paid for you with My own blood."

"John, are you OK?" I was staring at him, part in wonder, part in fright.

"I'm fine," he answered. "You get ready for bed. I'll be back in just a few minutes."

He went outside. The night air felt cool. The heavens were bright. John looked up in the star-studded sky. He wasn't alone. God was there. He could feel a divine presence, as close to him as the cigarettes in his shirt pocket.

That Bible verse about his body being the temple of God had hit him deep in his soul. He walked over to his car and opened the trunk where he stashed his beer and tobacco. He took them out and poured the beer on the ground. Then he opened the cigarette packs and crushed them in the dirt.

"All right, God," he declared as he fell down on his knees, "You win. I give myself to You. Please take these evils away from me. In the name of Jesus I claim the victory over them. Live in this temple as You have promised."

A peace washed over him. He quietly went inside and crawled in bed bedside me. I went to sleep in his arms. He could feel my abdomen against his side. The baby seemed to be traveling back and forth in its little house. His baby! The child of his flesh and blood. Could he provide all the security and love that their child needed?

Then he thought of his night on the town and the guys at work. They believed that shooting pool and drinking beer was real fun. He used to think so too. But somehow he had come home feeling empty and depressed. Now he knew why.

He remembered my prayer that snowy night when we had been stranded in the parking lot of the grocery store. He couldn't shake off the feeling that another Presence had been sitting with us. The car had started right after I prayed. And why did the verses that I read tonight cut through his soul? It was as if I knew all along what he was thinking. But I couldn't have—Grace had just brought the Bible lesson by that very day. That particular lesson was delivered just for him. God did have a personal interest in human affairs. God loved John Earnhardt enough to die for him; enough to want to dwell within him.

From then on John read the Bible every morning and night, and even on lunch breaks. The Bible opened up his mind and answered questions that had plagued him for years. When he read it, he felt a peace, an assurance that God was there with him. He felt direction in his life. All the while that same Spirit caused him to become more patient and more kind.

His problems didn't disappear overnight. Inside he still harbored a deep distrust of me. At church people hugged each other. He didn't like being hugged by others, and he didn't appreciate any males hugging me, regardless of how old they were. My smiles and laughter enraged him. Surely I was encouraging their attention!

In vain I tried to explain that it was just a physical demonstration of Christian love. It did not conjure up sexual implications to me. In his mind that was an outright lie. Finally, after one heated argument, I cried, "John, I am not your mother. I will not betray your trust in me."

It didn't sink in right away. Old habits and fears are easily aroused. But as we prayed together and studied, he began to build more trust in me and God. He discovered a wonderful Bible principle. Whatever you hold on to with your hands will slip away, but whatever you give to God will be eternal—even love. It wasn't a matter anymore of whether I was faithful to him. My loyalties to him weren't as important as my loyalties to Christ. He could see that I was developing a trustworthy character, and it all came from studying the Bible.

"'By beholding Him, we become changed,'" Grace had quoted to us one evening. "It's that way with everything. If you really love music and study music, then you become more musical. If you really study art, your brain is open to more artistic ways. When you behold Christ in His Word, you want to be more like Him. You find yourself doing things the way He would do them because you love Him, and His ways make more sense to you now. He covers you with His blood and character. He teaches you with His Holy Spirit. People have a tendency to behave like their heroes would behave."

"But Jesus is more than a hero," I added.

"Yes; He is our Savior—and He is our Lord," Grace explained.

John regularly joined his mother and me in the Bible studies. But it seemed to him that the more interest he showed, the less interest his mother showed.

"I believe in the Lord," Julia told us one evening as we discussed the questions at the dinner table. "But I can worship the Lord here at home. I don't think the Lord is as particular about what I do and where I go as y'all believe."

"In other words, Mother, you want to profess the Lord's name but live as you please," John told her. "Just as you always have."

"I taught you how to pray, Johnny." Her eyes took on a sharp glint. "I took you to church. I did the best I could."

"It's not about doing the best you can, Mom," John replied calmly, folding his napkin. "It's about giving your all to Christ.

Loving Him enough to be like Him. Letting Him be your Lord. When we ask God for forgiveness of all our sins and invite Him into our heart, it's more than just having His name on our lips. His blood covers your sins and gives you victory over them."

"Like you've gotten victory over cigarettes!" she sneered.

"You haven't seen me smoke in more than a week. Jesus has given me the complete victory."

Julia looked up from her plate.

I grinned at him over a forkful of spaghetti. "I noticed."

"You didn't say anything."

"Nope; I figured you would tell me when you wanted to."

John turned his attention back to Julia. "Mom, it's a wonderful feeling not to be chained to a pack of tobacco. And the best part is that I don't even crave it. I just knelt down and asked God to take it away from me. He did."

Julia shook her head. "I'll give you a week. You'll be smoking again. It's not that easy."

Chapter 17

John never smoked another cigarette. He never drank another beer, or any other kind of alcohol. Sometimes at night he would wake up with his hand close to his mouth, as though he was holding a cigarette, but he always remembered that God wanted to dwell in him. It didn't seem right to expect God to dwell within him with a pack of cigarettes in his shirt pocket, right next to his heart. So he copied Bible scriptures on blank business cards and tucked them in his shirt pocket. His favorite was Philippians 4:13: "I can do all things through Christ which strengtheneth me."

He was particularly fascinated with the books of Daniel and Revelation. To think that God loved His children so much that He wanted them to know every major event that would happen on Planet Earth! How carefully He had spelled out the prophecies concerning when Jesus would be born (Daniel 9) and when He would die. Why hadn't the Jews been able to see it?

In a dream from God, Nebuchadnezzar had seen which empires would rule the world throughout history. He had said, "There is a God in heaven that revealeth secrets, and maketh known to the king Nebuchadnezzar what shall be in the latter days" (Daniel 2:28).

People *had* to be told. If only they understood the prophecies, then they would recognize Satan's deceptions and be prepared for the second coming of Jesus. They would begin reading the Bible and going to church.

The conviction settled on him that he must be the one to take it to his family and friends. He decided that since his mom and dad weren't listening to him, maybe his friends would. His high school friends, Tony and David, would surely be impressed when they heard his testimony of how the Lord had changed his life. They had grown up together. They had hunted, partied, and shared their deepest thoughts with each other. Since his marriage, he really hadn't spent much time with them. So with Bible in hand, he drove to see them.

Blond-haired Tony came out to meet him with a big smile on his face. "Man, it's good to see you! How's married life?"

The two talked about school, friends, and jobs. Finally John could wait no longer. "Tony," he said, "I want to tell you what the good Lord has been doing for me." He then proceeded to tell Tony about his decision to accept Jesus as his Savior.

Tony's smile froze on his face. He had to hold his lips apart and at an angle to keep from showing his amusement. When John offered him an invitation to study the Bible with him, he held up his hands. "No, John. I have plenty of time for religion. I'm going to wait till I get older, like when I get married."

David's initial reaction was shock, but once it wore off he promised to look into the Bible and at least attend one church service with John.

John decided to visit one of his other friends. Terry played in a rock and roll band, had hair down to the middle of his back, and kept a string of girls following after him as if he were some big superstar.

Terry wasn't very receptive. "What kind of drug did you take?" he blurted.

John could hardly believe his friends' response. "They acted as if God was an optional commodity," he told me. "They thought I was nuts!"

"You didn't accept it the first time, either," I reminded him. "Just keep working with them, and let them see Jesus in your life."

The men at work didn't even mention God unless it was in foul language or sacrilegious jokes. John could hardly stand to be in their presence. But he patiently prayed for the Lord to give him experiences to share with them. But instead of discovering a Bible truth, they used it to begin debates on religious issues.

"Maybe you shouldn't talk about the Bible so much," I advised him. "Be a living sermon to them."

"That's probably true," he admitted, "but I think God has another plan for me. I feel that He is calling me to work for Him full-time. I keep having dreams, and in every dream I'm standing in front of a large group of people. I think I'm going to become a Methodist minister."

■ ■ ■

Julia, John, and I began going to the little White Methodist church each Sunday. As the size of the congregation had dropped to about 35, they were thrilled to have young blood in their midst. Before long John was teaching Sunday school and sometimes preaching when the minister couldn't be there.

There were several things that bothered him, though. Christ had given him victory over smoking, and it seemed that his minister could hardly wait for his own sermon to end so he could go outside and smoke a cigarette. And when John talked with him about the prophecies of Daniel, he just grunted.

"John," the minister told him one evening as they sat visiting in the living room. "Just love God and do the best you can. Forget all this other stuff."

"But why did God put the prophecies in the Bible if we aren't suppose to understand them?" John asked.

The minister shrugged. "I'll be honest with you—I don't know. Besides, I really need to go home."

John watched him as he walked out the door and lit up a cigarette on the front porch. He wondered if the man really had to leave, or if he just had to have a cigarette and felt embarrassed lighting one up in front of him.

He wished they could have talked longer. He had so many questions. If his own minister couldn't answer them, then who could? Immediately he thought of Grace.

Chapter 18

That week Grace gave us a Bible study that had the effect of a bomb bursting in the air. She gave us a study on the fourth commandment.

"*Remember the sabbath day, to keep it holy.*

"*Six days shalt thou labour, and do all thy work:*

"*But the seventh day is the sabbath of the Lord thy God: in it thou shalt not do any work, thou, nor thy son, nor thy daughter, thy manservant, nor thy maidservant, nor thy cattle, nor thy stranger that is within thy gates:*

"*For in six days the Lord made heaven and earth, the sea, and all that in them is, and rested the seventh day: wherefore the Lord blessed the sabbath day, and hallowed it*" (Exodus 20:8-11).

When Grace explained that the seventh day was Saturday, not Sunday, we all fell quiet. None of us had even heard of a church that kept Saturday for the Sabbath, other than the Jews. Didn't the change of days have something to do with the resurrection?

John studied the topic thoroughly before he discussed it with anyone. I came to the conclusion that yes, Saturday was the Sabbath, but I didn't really see the need for changing churches or refraining from worldly fun that day. What difference did it make? I had been a Methodist all my life, and I truly loved the Lord.

Grace answered each one of our objections with a Bible text. "'If ye love me, keep my commandments' [John 14:15]. Remember that Jesus is to be Lord of your life. He doesn't command us to do something just because He wants to rule over us."

She then proceeded to tell the story of how sin began in heaven with the most beautiful angel who worked closest to God. "Thou wast perfect in thy ways from the day that thou wast created, till iniquity was found in thee. . . . Thine heart was lifted up because of thy beauty, thou hast corrupted thy wisdom by reason of thy brightness' [Ezekiel, 28:15-17]. 'How art thou fallen from heaven, O Lucifer, son of the morning! . . . For thou hast said in thine heart, I will ascend into heaven, I will exalt my throne above the stars of God' [Isaiah 14:12, 13].

"God doesn't force anyone to obey Him," Grace said. "Lucifer wanted more power, even though he already was the most beautiful and powerful angel in heaven. According to Revelation 12:9, he was cast out of heaven, and his goal is to deceive the world. As humans we must choose whom we will serve—God, who is good—or Satan who is evil. Remember the verse, 'If ye love me, keep my commandments' [John 14:15]? It's not a matter of trying to work your way into heaven, as some claim. Rather, it's a matter of choosing whom you will serve. God doesn't give a partial package. It's all or none. It was that way with His most powerful angel, and it was that way with Adam and Eve.

"God gave us no room to say we don't understand," Grace went on. "Some people teach that Paul claimed that the law was done away with, as if Paul had the power to change the words of Jesus. The truth is, they harmonize with each other. The ceremonial laws pertaining to killing animals for sacrifices was nailed to the cross because Jesus' death fulfilled those laws."

"But we don't know what day is the Sabbath," Julia shot back. "The calendars have been changed."

"The seven-day weekly cycle has never been changed. Look up 'Saturday' in the dictionary," Grace suggested. "In almost every language it means 'Sabbath,' or 'seventh day.'"

"But how was it changed?" John wanted to know.

Grace took a small tan paperback book out of her purse. "This is *The Convert's Catechism of Catholic Doctrine,*" she said, holding it up for all of them to see. "On page 50 it tells how the Sabbath was changed. Read it aloud, John."

John cleared his throat and took the book:

"'Q. What is the Third Commandment?

"'A. The Third Commandment is: Remember that thou keep holy the Sabbath day.

"'Q. Which is the Sabbath day?

"'A. Saturday is the Sabbath day.

"'Q. Why do we observe Sunday instead of Saturday?

"'A. We observe Sunday instead of Saturday because the Catholic Church transferred the solemnity from Saturday to Sunday. . . .

"'Q. By what authority did the Church substitute Sunday for Saturday?

"'A. The Church substituted Sunday for Saturday by the plenitude of that divine power which Jesus Christ bestowed upon her.'"

John put the book down, his face a mirror of surprise. "I didn't know that's how it happened!" he exclaimed. "Why did other Christians go along with it?"

"It didn't happen overnight," Grace explained. "It was a very slow process. The Catholic Church wanted to extend the gospel to the heathen and unite. They kept Sunday in honor of the sun god. It started out as small compromises, a kind of give and take for the sake of unity."

"But God wrote the Ten Commandments in stone with His own hand," I commented. "And I read today that Jesus said He wouldn't change even a jot or tittle from the law. That's the dotting of an i or the crossing of a t," I explained to Julia, who was looking at Grace with amazement. "Here, I'll read it to you." I opened my Bible.

"'Think not that I am come to destroy the law, or the prophets: I am not come to destroy, but to fulfil. For verily I say unto you, Till heaven and earth pass, one jot or one tittle shall in no wise pass from the law, till all be fulfilled. Whosoever therefore shall break one of these least commandments, and shall teach men so, he shall be called the least in the kingdom of heaven: but whosoever shall do and teach them, the same shall be called great in the kingdom of heaven'" [Matthew 5:17-19].

"The first few chapters of the Bible tell how God gave Adam and Eve a choice of obedience," Grace reminded us. "They were told not to eat the fruit from the tree of good and evil. Banishment from the

Garden of Eden and eventual death would be the end result. And when they chose to disobey, that's what they received. They were forever banned from partaking of the tree of life, which meant death. That tree of life was their connection with immortality. They slowly began to die. We can read about that in the second and third chapters of Genesis.

"The last chapter of the Bible reminds us that disobedience is what caused the separation from the tree of life. 'Blessed are they that do his commandments, that they may have *right* to the *tree of life*' (Revelation 22:14).

"So," Grace concluded, "always remember that the beginning and the end of the Bible couples obedience with the tree of life. Only those who choose to love God with their whole heart will obey Him. When Adam and Eve were created, they were created in the likeness of God (Genesis 1:26). They lost that likeness through disobedience. Eve really believed the words of Satan, but her belief didn't save her from the penalty of sin. The law of God restores that likeness because it is the character of God."

"That's deep!" I exclaimed. "I don't feel as though I can be that obedient."

"You can't," Grace said. "Neither can I, in my own power." She turned to John 15 and read: "'Abide in me, and I in you. As the branch cannot bear fruit of itself, except it abide in the vine; no more can ye, except ye abide in me' [verse 4]. Only in Christ," she repeated. "John said it this way: 'But as many as received him, to them gave he power to become the sons of God, even to them that believe on his name' [John 1:12].

"We must give our heart to Jesus daily," Grace emphasized. "We cannot perfectly walk the Christian life any more than a baby can walk the first week of their life. A baby grows, and so does a Christian. A baby falls, and so does a Christian. Eventually a baby learns to stand on their own two feet, but a Christian never does. A Christian stands on Christ alone.

"Oh, and by the way," she concluded, "the last chapter of the Bible declares that anyone who tries to take away (or change) the Scriptures will be taken out of the book of life and receive the plagues" (Revelation 22:18:19).

Both John and I began to study earnestly and prayed that God would always live in us. The more we studied the Bible, the more we realized that the Sabbath had a deeper significance than simply going to church. It was not a day of idle rest. The Sabbath was a block in time given to humankind for the purpose of rediscovering our roots, like a weekly call home. God created us; He wanted to dwell in us. One day He would come back for us. The Sabbath helped us to know who we were and where we were going. That very fact made us more conscious of our actions and deeds. People, we concluded, who thought they climbed out of a slime pit didn't mind living in one, and their actions reflected it.

Clifford Goldstein summed it up this way in his book *A Pause for Peace:*

"In true Sabbathkeeping, we are so free and secure in Christ that we can put aside the secular for 24 hours and pursue the spiritual instead. By keeping the Sabbath we express that we are in the world but not of it, because for that day we can tune out the world and tune in God. Sabbathkeeping shows that we are not so trapped by the mundane, that it doesn't have such a grip on us, that we cannot weekly slip away from it to spend quality time with Christ. Adherence to the fourth commandment reveals that we have enough trust in Jesus to temporarily suspend our ambitions (though others around us forge ahead) and rest in Christ, enjoying the freedom that comes from faith that God will provide."

From then on I declared that the Sabbath experience not only healed us spiritually; it gave us emotional healing as well. The emotional healing provided us a stronger base for our marriage and opened our eyes to each other's needs and the needs of others.

As John read the Bible he found that there were hundreds of blessings promised to those who would keep His commandments.

Solomon wrote: "My son, forget not my law; but let thine heart keep my commandments; for length of days, and long life, and peace, shall they add to thee. Let not mercy and truth forsake thee: bind them about thy neck; write them upon the table of thine heart" (Proverbs 3:1-3).

Just as God wrote them on tables of stone, John added to himself, *we are to write them upon the table of our heart.*

In the New Testament Jesus said, "If ye keep my commandments, ye shall abide in my love; even as I have kept my Father's commandments, and abide in his love" (John 15:10).

Paul wrote, "For not the hearers of the law are just before God, but the doers of the law shall be justified" (Romans 2:13).

"And whatsoever we ask, we receive of him, because we keep his commandments, and do those things that are pleasing in his sight" (1 John 3:22).

As John quoted these texts to his family and friends, they called him a legalist. "Haven't you heard of grace in the Bible?" they asked.

"Yes," John answered them. "It is extended to everyone who loves God with their whole heart. Did I ever tell you about my first speeding ticket?" he asked as if changing the subject. He looked at their bewildered faces. "Well, let me tell you about it. I had just gotten my first car—a 1955 metallic blue Chevy. I wanted to impress my date that night, so I did a little drag racing on Main Street. I guess I had gotten up to about 85 miles an hour when I saw the flashing lights in my rearview mirror.

"The policeman strutted up to my car. I won't repeat all the bad things he said, but when he got through swearing, he told me that if he put 85 on my ticket I would lose my license."

"You deserved it," his mother chimed in.

"Yeah, I reckon I did; but I was young and stupid."

"Still are," someone murmured.

John ignored their good-natured fun and continued the story. "I had just gotten my license, so I pleaded with the office to have mercy. He told me that he would write 50 instead of 85. That meant a big fine—but I'd keep my license. That police officer showed mercy to me."

He paused a moment so his next words would take effect. "Now, what would have happened if I had gotten in the car and zoomed off, going 85 miles an hour again?"

"They'd popped you in jail," the group chorused.

"Yeah, you're right," John agreed. "Mercy isn't an excuse for breaking the law, is it?"

The whole group fell silent. What was there to say?

Chapter 19

Angela Christine Earnhardt was born on a cold Sabbath afternoon in January. It was the first Sabbath that John didn't go to church since studying that topic. My blood pressure shot up during delivery, and I went into convulsions. The baby was breach, making the delivery so difficult that I almost died. We would always feel that God directly intervened and saved my life.

John and I were baptized a few months later. We wanted to make a public confession of Jesus Christ and realized that baptism was a symbol of burying the old life of sin and being resurrected as a new creature in Christ Jesus. Ruth Oliver and her husband, Dr. Joseph Oliver, who 19 years before had delivered John in the back of the tavern, witnessed our baptism. The nurse's prayer had been answered.

A few weeks before John's baptism, Skip Culpepper, a publishing director of HHES (Home Health Education Service), convinced John that he could begin a ministry of winning people to the Lord by selling Christian books. To do so, John realized that he must sell Betsy, his 1955 Chevy, because he would need a car that got better gas mileage. So he bought a Ford Falcon and became a literature evangelist, traveling from county to county, spreading the good news of God's grace. John was truly a traveler for the Lord. That same year Dale Earnhardt was driving a Ford Falcon in racing.

Three years later John began having the dream again. He was always standing in front of a large group of people. One day he shared that dream with a traveling evangelist named Buddy Brass. Many people called him Machine Gun Buddy because he could shoot so many Bible verses out of his head from memory as he preached.

"John," he said, walking over to a chalkboard, "you have a choice." He wrote the words "selling books" on the board. "You can sell books all your life, and you might work your way into the pastoral ministry." He then wrote "college" on the board. "You can go to college and get a degree, and you will definitely become a pastor. Which route is the shortest? Which will guarantee you an opportunity to preach?"

"I can't afford college," John said.

"If God wants you there, He will make a way," Buddy replied. "Let's pray about it."

While John was struggling with the decision to step out in faith and go to college, his little brother Rondy was struggling with a battle of his own. Now a teenager, the family felt as though a stranger had taken Rondy's place. He painted the ceiling in his bedroom black, and added splashes of psychedelic paint. Then he retreated to his room and seldom spoke with anyone in the family. When he did speak it was usually a yes or no. If pressed for an explanation, he would respond with an ugly outburst of temper

Since he wouldn't talk to anyone, John left little notes under his door, assuring him that everything was going to be all right if he would just turn his problems over to God. Rondy never acknowledged the messages from John. He completely ignored his own father, and when the two did speak it was usually in anger.

James Earnhardt was at a loss as to how to handle this problem. He had never been a good communicator, but he did expect more than a grunt out of his son. He clearly suspected drugs, but couldn't prove it. The uglier things got at home, the more he retreated to his 18-wheeler.

During the time Rondy was battling his problems, Julia found someone's credit card, and she and her sister went from store to store on a wild spending spree. John felt that something strange was happening when she bought him a silk tie for church and it wasn't even Christmas or his birthday. Everyone wondered how she could afford all the new household items, clothes, and trinkets that suddenly graced the house.

Then one evening Jean received a phone call from the police.

Julia had failed to show up for court for the charge of illegal use of the credit card. Would she come and sign for her mother's release? When James discovered his wife's crime, he became so angry that he took her name off his bank account and refused to give her any money. Now the two of them couldn't speak without yelling.

Not long after that, Julia received a phone call in the middle of the night. Another truck driver had failed to see a stop sign and had plowed into James's truck. James was thrown through the windshield and out on the pavement under the other truck. The wheel stopped within inches of his head. She rushed to the hospital and found him unconscious in the intensive-care unit. The doctors offered little hope. In tears, she called her children to come see their father.

It was a sad group that gathered around the hospital bed. Convulsions racked the battered body before them. Nurses strapped his wrists and arms to the bedside rails in an effort to protect the tubes that entered his nostrils and veins. The doctor explained that James had suffered extensive head injuries. He did not expect him to regain consciousness, and if he did, he would never be the same again.

While the thought of losing her husband crushed Julia, she thought about the financial ruin she would be in if James died. Because he had taken her name off the bank account, she would not be able to get one penny out of the bank.

"May I have his wallet and personal items found on the truck?" she asked.

The nurse nodded, and the two left the room, leaving John and Rondy alone, standing on either side of the bed.

"Dad may not live," John told his brother. "Don't you want to make peace with him now?"

Remorse and sorrow were evident on Rondy's face. He nodded and bent low to his father's ear. "Please forgive me," he whispered. "I am so sorry for the way I've treated you."

There was no response from the now-still form. The thought of his father dying without peace between them filled Rondy with anguish. "Dad!" he cried. "I love you. You've got to hear me. You've got to! Listen to me!" He gently reached for the rough, grease-stained hand closest to him and held it tenderly. "If you can hear me and will forgive me, please squeeze my hand."

It was quiet in the room, so quiet that all John could hear was the occasional beep and suctioning sounds of the machine by the bed. Their eyes were riveted to the hands strapped to the bed rail. Then slowly, ever so slowly, their father's fingers tightened around Rondy's hand.

■ ■ ■

Julia didn't witness the joyous reuniting of hearts in the next room. She numbly signed the papers and collected the little bag containing his wallet, checkbook, pocketknife, and comb. The doctor had all but said she would be a widow in a few short hours. The house wasn't even paid for. She didn't know what kind of life insurance he had, if any. How dare he die on her and leave her penniless! What was she supposed to do? How could she get out of this mess?

She remembered their last fight and his unforgiving rebuke over her arrest. If only he had tried to understand what it was like to sit at home alone night after night. She had reached out to him, hoping against hope that he would take her in his arms and hold her, the way he used to. But he had turned a cold shoulder her way and stalked out of the room.

She felt so alone. Her parents were dead. Her sister, who had been in on the whole credit card scheme, had fled the scene. Her children acted ashamed of her—yet almost everything that she had gotten with that credit card had been for them.

They honestly acted as if they loved James more than her, even though it was she who had worked her fingers to the bone taking care of them when they were little and operating the grill at the same time. It was *she* who had changed their diapers and bought their Christmas presents. It was *she* who had rushed them to the doctor when they were sick and took care of them.

He had wooed her away from the father of her children. He had drifted in with a cocky grin and somehow stole her heart from the man who loved her more than anyone had loved her. He had actually bought her alcohol, and then blamed her for drinking it. It was *James's* idea to close the Grill, her only means of support. *He* wanted to drive that horrible truck and drag them from state to state.

She had always struggled to keep ahead, and the stress of it had led her to drink and, yes, to steal. Why didn't he try to understand? Why would he deprive her of equality with the checking account? That money was as much hers as his. Once he was dead the bank account could be frozen for weeks. She had to think of a way to get that money out of the bank.

"Mom, are you OK?"

Julia looked up to see Jean, Jimmy, and Judy standing beside her.

"How's Daddy?"

Julia shook her head. "Not good. Why don't you go in there and see him? Johnny and Rondy are in there."

She fumbled through the little bag of items the nurse had given her. She read through his account to see whom he had written checks to and how much money he had in the account. She knew he had money in more than one bank, but she didn't know where.

James had left her no choice. She grabbed a pen and wrote out a check for cash, writing as nearly as she could to resemble his handwriting. She would leave a little money in the account to avoid suspicion from the bank teller.

Her head was aching from thinking so much, and rumbles in her stomach reminded her that she hadn't eaten in hours. She stared at the forged check and wondered how she could cash it. She couldn't leave the hospital now. The banks were closed for the night anyway. But what if he died before she could get to the bank?

John walked into the room. "Is there anything you need, Mom?" he asked.

"Yes," she told him, as a new thought entered her mind. John didn't know that James had taken her name off the account. "Johnny, I need you to cash this check. I can't leave your daddy now. I need to stay here with him. Take it to the bank the first thing in the morning. This is awfully important to me, son."

John put the check in his wallet without looking at it. "All right," he agreed. "I'll cash it. Now why don't you go in with him for a while?"

Throughout the night the family took turns going in to see James. At one point when Julia was out of the room, John pulled the check out of his wallet.

"This is for more than gas money!" he exclaimed as he showed the check to Jean and Jimmy. "What has Mom got up her sleeve?"

It seemed that each of them had bits of the story and, when put together, they figured out what had happened. If Dad died, Mom would be in trouble. But if he lived, and found out they had turned over his money to her and she had squandered it, they would be in trouble. Dad would never forgive them.

"Go ahead and cash the check," the others agreed. "But don't give the money to Mom. Put it in your own bank account, or open a new one where you can have access to the money. If Dad dies, then give the money to Mom. If not, then hold it for him."

"Mom will never forgive me for this," John worried.

The others shook their heads in sympathy. It put their brother in a hard spot. Bucking Mom was not be taken lightly. Under the circumstances, though, it would be the best thing to do.

The next day when John returned to the hospital, Julia was obviously relieved to see him. But when he informed her of their decision, her dark eyes flashed in anger. "I can't believe you'd do this to me," she spat at him. "You'll be sorry for crossing me, Johnny. I'm telling you right now that you'll be sorry if you don't give that money to me."

"Mom, you are so upset you really don't know what you're doing. Dad is going to live. He would never forgive you if you spent his money."

"I wasn't going to waste it!" she shot back. "But I will eventually need it to pay the bills. Who is going to keep food on the table and the electricity paid up while he lies here?"

"I'll pay those bills with the money if we need to," John informed her.

"I just want you to know that you are out of my will!" She

turned her back to him and stared at the wall. How could her own children distrust her so?

John walked over and looked at his father. If Dad did come out of this coma, what a mess he would wake up to!

■ ■ ■

James Earnhardt was in a coma for three weeks. Julia faithfully sat by his bedside day after day and night after lonely night. She had plenty of time to think. She thought about her mama and papa. Yes, Papa had a drinking problem. He wasn't perfect, but she loved him and he loved her. When she was little he had consented for her to have a parrot. She named it Polly. Polly died when neighborhood children fed her a biscuit. So Julia had the parrot stuffed, and it was still in her den, perched on a little swing hanging from the ceiling.

She thought about her first husband, James Fatata, an Italian from New York. He was a good man who seemed to worship the ground she walked on. He had given her three beautiful, dark-eyed children. If only he hadn't left her alone so much. But he was in the Army, and there wasn't much choice. She hated to be alone.

Then happy-go-lucky James Earnhardt entered her life. He was daring and had a reckless attitude that nearly drove her mad. His presence took her breath away. At times he was warm, and at times he was aloof. She couldn't quite figure him out, but decided she'd spend the rest of her life trying to.

Where had they gone wrong, the two of them? What had caused her to drown some nameless demon within her with whiskey? She hadn't done it alone; James drank, too. The difference was he could stop; she couldn't.

Or could she?

A growing desire filled her heart. A voice seemed to whisper to her that she didn't have to live her life in bitterness and regret. She was weak, but God was strong. "Dear Lord," she prayed, "I don't want to drink anymore. Please help me! I don't want my children to hate me. I don't want my husband to mistrust me."

Even as she prayed she felt a craving for a drink. Her hands shook as she reached into her purse and pulled out a bottle of nerve medicine. Surely this would help. She would rely on that nerve medicine in the following months of slow recovery.

The man who walked out of that hospital was not the same man she had married. His patience was not more than an inch long, and his train of thought just didn't seem to be the same. Nevertheless, she stuck by his side and put up with his searing tongue and pacing restlessness. Fortunately, her children rallied around. The accident had forced them all to stand together.

John was especially thankful when he could withdraw all the money from his bank and hand it to his father. It took some time for James to get back on his feet, but eventually he began making short trips in his truck.

And Julia stuck by her promise to God. She never drank another drop of alcohol.

Chapter 20

John could never fully dismiss Buddy Brass's words about going to college. He knew God wanted him to be a minister. The calling was like a flame in his heart that continually burned. He tried to extinguish it in another type of ministry, but it only burned brighter. He even tried to reason with God. "How can I go to college when I can barely afford to pay my bills now?" But God always whispered back, "Follow me."

God did own the world. Surely He could make a way for John to go to college. He asked the local pastor, Elder Henry Fowler, to pray for them. Elder Fowler encouraged him to speak to the publishing company to see if they offered any scholarships. In the meantime, he allowed John to preach occasionally.

The women of the small church did their best to nurture our growing family. Various ones invited us home on Sabbath for lunch. I was able to taste healthful cooking and get the recipes. The head deacon, Hurley Bowers, and his wife, Rose, fed us many a meal. Thelma Lombard, Ruth Oliver's sister-in-law, visited frequently or invited me to go shopping. Without realizing it, this small group of believers taught us through example how to cook, raise children, and worship.

Their instruction came at a good time. Little blond-haired Angie was only 14 months old when I realized I was pregnant again. That fall John and one of the deacon's sons, Larry Bowers, decided to hold their own evangelistic series and take turns preaching. They made homemade posters and tacked them up around town. They enlisted the help of church members to personally invite everyone in the neighborhood.

After each meeting Pastor Fowler took them aside and critiqued their sermons. "John," he said one evening after John had referred to the patriarch Job, "it's not *job*, as in a place of work; it's *Job*."

John repeated it several times correctly. "OK, OK; I got it," he assured the minister. Another evening John referred to Acts 2:29 in his sermon. Later Pastor Fowler told him, "It's not *sculpture*; it's *sepulchre*."

"OK, OK; I got it," John assured him again.

"He couldn't pronounce half the words," Elder Fowler said later, "but what he lacked in knowledge, he made up for in enthusiasm."

Toward the end of the meetings, I didn't feel good and wanted to take a night off. Since I was due at any time, I decided to ask Julia to stay with me at home while John conducted the meeting. Months before Grandma and Grandpa Earnhardt had decided to get rid of their old farmhouse and buy a mobile home. Julia paid to have the old house moved to the very spot where John had been born. The old tavern had long since been torn down, replaced by a new one that was built half a mile up the road. After it was set up John and I moved in and paid Julia rent each month.

So Julia came down to spend Friday evening with Angie and me while John preached. It was an old house with lots of dark corners in the closets. While Julia sat on the couch and knitted, little Angie played on the floor. Eventually, she became restless and begged for another toy. I went into the closet to see what I could find to amuse the toddler. I saw a paper bag on the shelf and without thinking I stuck my hand inside to see what was in it. A quick prick sent me running to Julia, bag in hand.

"I just got bit by a spider in this bag!" I complained.

"Let me see," Julia said, taking the bag from me and emptying the contents. A speck of black fuzz tumbled out. "Why, it's nothing," she assured me. She reached out to touch it, and it moved! Suddenly eight legs stretched out and the small red hourglass on its abdomen was plain to see. A black widow spider! I grabbed a mason jar, and between the two of us, we trapped it.

"We've got to get you to the doctor!" Julia exclaimed. "That spider is poisonous. Already a red line was moving up my arm.

"I can't afford another doctor bill," I worried. "I'm just going to pray." I fell on my knees and asked the Lord to take care of me.

Julia stared at me in disbelief. "Pray!" she exclaimed. "You've got to get to Dr. Lombard."

I shook my head, my lips still moving silently. Finally I opened my eyes. "Can't do that. Dr. Lombard and Dr. Oliver are in the meeting with John. If one of us goes in, John will think the baby is coming and won't be able to finish the sermon. Whatever we do, we can't interrupt a sermon. Don't worry; the Lord will take care of me."

Julia headed for the phone. "I'll call Dr. Lombard's brother. He's close enough to the meeting hall that he can walk in and talk to her, and John won't suspect a thing."

Fifteen minutes later Dr. Lombard drove up with medicine in hand. The red line had spread up my arm. "I've never known of anyone dying from a black widow spider bite, but you are pregnant, and it won't hurt to be sure," she said as she gave me a shot in the arm.

Julia sat on the couch with her legs tucked up underneath her, holding Angie in her arms. "I suppose if I was having a heart attack you'd kneel down and pray," she scoffed.

"Well, that would be the first thing I'd do," I admitted.

Julia groaned while Dr. Lombard stood there and grinned.

One year and 11 months after the birth of Angie, a second little girl, Tamera Renee, arrived on December 22. On Christmas Day John and I drove home, stopping briefly on the way to let the Bowers see our new little dark-haired beauty.

John tried to comfort me when I lamented that I didn't have but one little doll for Angie's Christmas. "I guess a sister is enough present for Angie. She's too young to know anything about holidays."

John's sister Jean, who was now married, met us at our house with a beautiful little play table and chairs, coloring books and crayons, and a little coat and hat for Angie. Somehow she knew there was no money for Christmas presents, and she filled in the void with her own money. I never forgot that kindness. That one act endeared Jean to me more than she would ever know.

■ ■ ■

College plans had to be put on hold. If God wanted us there, He would have to help us financially. It took all our money to pay the doctor bills, rent, and utilities. Sometimes we didn't have enough left over for groceries. On one such occasion we looked into the empty cupboards and prayed. That very evening Grace knocked on the door, holding a big basket of food in her arms.

"We had some food left over when we made Christmas baskets," she told us. "Thought you could use some extra food."

She had no idea that the "extra food" was heaven-sent.

That summer John found out he could go on a scholarship program with HHES. The problem was that the company held all the money earned on commissions until the end of the summer. Then they would add a percentage, the local conference would add a percentage, and it would be sent to the college, which also added a percentage for tuition. In that way his commissions were more than doubled. It was a total act of faith to go three months without a paycheck. Like Gideon of old, John and I hung out the "fleece." John's prayer was "Lord, if You want me to go to college, please provide the first year of tuition."

As soon as he went on the scholarship program, his sales tripled. People shared garden produce. Gifts of clothes and money came from unexpected sources. By summer's end John had sold enough books to pay for the first year of college. He now had no doubt as to where God wanted him to be.

He went to his former high school principal to ask for a transcript of records. As soon as he walked in the office the man backed up against the wall and held up his hands in defense.

John reached out to shake hands with the principal. "I'm a Christian now," he told him. "I want to apologize for all the trouble I caused you." He told him about his scholarship and how he was going to be a minister.

The principal was plainly relieved. "John, you don't want your transcripts. No college would accept you if they read what was on your records. My advice is to tell them that they are unavailable."

Later he approached his father. "Dad, would you haul our furniture and belongings up to the college in your truck?" Another young couple in the church was going to the same school and wanted to know if James could transport their things, too. Much to everyone's relief, he agreed.

So with a $200 farewell gift from our little home church, John and I packed our belongings and headed off to Southern Missionary College in Tennessee. As we were pulling out of the drive, Alice Bradford, one of the church members, drove up and handed us two beautiful dolls for the girls. "It might be a while before they get any new toys," she explained. "Maybe they will remember us when they play with them."

That small church made disciples of John and me without even realizing it. They took us into their homes and taught us by example how to change our life by changing our lifestyle. Those little acts of kindness were never forgotten—and will be repaid. One day the Lord will tally the records. Christ promises, "Inasmuch as ye have done it unto one of the least of these my brethren, ye have done it unto me" (Matthew 25:40).

Chapter 21

As soon as John arrived on campus he went into the business office and informed the secretary that he was there to study for the ministry. He had no transcripts and no high school diploma. The first thing they did was give him a GED test.

John silently prayed, then took the test. He passed.

Next, they gave him an ACT test. "Well, I can act," he joked nervously with the sober-faced teacher.

As he glanced over the sheets of questions, he realized that he didn't know any of the answers. "O God," he prayed, quoting King David and applying it to himself, "You are my 'refuge and strength, a very present help in trouble' [Psalm 46:1]. Please guide my pencil." He didn't bother to read most of the questions. The directions indicated he was to choose A, B, C, or D for an answer. He simply randomly chose a letter from each question, then handed the paper in.

God must have guided his pencil. He made a high score on the ACT that he didn't even read. There was no doubt in his mind that God wanted him there.

His first job was working for the town, answering the phone for the ambulance and fire department. The chief of police resented John's request to be off on Sabbath, reminding him that it's OK to do well on the Sabbath and that he must take his turn to work every other weekend.

Since the ambulance and fire department could no more close down than could a hospital, John reported in when he was scheduled. However, after the first week his conscience bothered him. Many non-Christian employees were coming in and filling out forms and doing work that John felt was nonessential. He told the boss that he would not work on Sabbath anymore.

When he went back to get his work schedule the secretary informed him that he was fired. "Will you put the reason down on paper for me?" he asked.

"No. You know why, and I know why," she answered.

Word leaked out on campus that a new student with two kids had lost his job for not working on Sabbath. Within three days a Mr. Myers knocked on his door. "I could use someone like you to be a night watchman," he told John. He offered him more pay and better hours than he had made working for the town—and he didn't have to work on Sabbath. Through all these experiences we learned to put our trust in God, not humanity.

We also learned that one will find within any church or organization, no matter how holy, people who do not behave as Christians should. There will be some teachers—and even ministers—who are not converted. We cannot look at others. We must do as Christ admonished Peter: "What is that to thee? follow thou me" (John 21:22).

"I made up my mind that I was there to get a Christian education," John said later. "As in all large institutions, you find truly converted teachers and students who are doing their best to follow Jesus. Satan will have his own group, just to mess it up for the Christians. I decided to take everything to God in prayer, do what I was supposed to do, and not worry about the other."

Prof. Douglas Bennett, who was the head of the Religion Department, helped John organize a series of Bible studies that could be used as a Bible marking guide and an excellent resource for Bible studies.

When John left Southern College, he went straight to Wildwood Sanitarium and Hospital, a small self-supporting school in the mountains bordering Tennessee and Georgia. He wanted to see both sides of the work, the self-supporting and the organized. He came to the conclusion that God was leading both groups in a miraculous way. They were both different but equally important. After three months of study at Wildwood, he received a call to be a

Bible worker in a church in Hagerstown, Maryland (thanks to Douglas Bennett at Southern College) where he gave Bible studies full-time. The Lord blessed with so many baptisms that Elder Bill May, president of the Chesapeake Conference, requested that he pastor two churches on the Eastern Shore of Maryland. At last he was fulfilling the dream to preach!

■ ■ ■

While John was fulfilling his dream to preach, Dale Earnhardt was slowly building his dream of becoming a full-time race car driver. His father, Ralph, had died of a heart attack in 1973 while rebuilding a carburetor. The family buried him in a small cemetery in Kannapolis and had a race car carved on his tombstone.

And that was the legacy Ralph left for Dale—racing. His mother gave him the two cars in the garage that his father had competed in. It was a sad event, but it proved to be the turning point in Dale's career. Dale was forced to make it on his own, and it wasn't easy. "I'd give up everything I got if he were still alive," he would say later, "but I don't think I'd be where I am if he hadn't died."

He worked as a welder and mechanic and raced on the weekends. He'd borrow money during the week to buy racing tires and parts, in hopes of winning a race that weekend to pay it back. "Racing cost me my second marriage because of the things I took away from my family," he said. But out of those two marriages came two sons, Kerry and Dale, Jr., and a daughter named Kelly.

Dale fine-tuned his skill by driving with pinpoint accuracy, plucking pieces of ivy off the wall with his car. He learned to put a car in places that most drivers wouldn't go. His big break came in 1978 when an owner named Will Cronkrite lost a driver. Dale was asked to fill in the position, and raced for four races. He finished seventh in one of them, which gave him the recognition he needed.

His daring attitude won the admiration of the crowds. At one race in Atlanta an 11-year veteran driver, Dave Marcis, smacked Earnhardt in the door. Fearlessly Earnhardt banged him right back. Crowds soon learned that Dale was all about winning. In order to win he provoked scrapes and spun out other cars, re-gardless of who they were, teammates or best friends.

He put the fun back into the sport of racing. NASCAR fans ei-ther loved him or hated him. But most loved him. He had come from the bottom with nothing but sheer determination. After winning the Winston Cup Rookie of the Year, he quickly climbed the ladder to fame, one race at a time. He was the first driver to win the points championship the very next season after winning the rookie award.

John kept up with Dale's career. He wanted so badly to share what the Lord had done for him. Finally he decided to write him a letter:

> Dear Dale,
>
> It's been a long time since we played around my father's racetrack in Gold Hill. Our paths have surely gone in different directions! You are doing exactly what you've always wanted to do. Congratulations on your recent wins!
>
> I want to share with you what has happened in my life. Just a few years ago I became a Christian. Words can't ex-press what a difference Jesus Christ has made in my life and in my marriage. I don't know what your relationship with the Lord is, but I can testify that He has made a dif-ference in this Carolina boy. I'm enclosing some material that I've found helpful.
>
> John Earnhardt

Staring at the envelope in his hand, John prayed that it would touch Dale's life; then he dropped it in the mailbox to travel the 400 miles that separated them. John thought all afternoon about Dale, who had won championship after championship, making more money in one year than John hoped to see in a lifetime.

A few weeks later an envelope from Dale arrived. In it was an autographed picture of him, standing in front of his car. But no comment about the Lord.

Chapter 22

While John loved serving the Lord as a pastor, there were certain duties he could have done without. Funerals were one of them. While he found fulfillment in being available for his church members at those times they suffered heart-wrenching sorrow, at the same time he wondered if there was more he could have said or done to comfort them. And the traditional sermons that most pastors preached were enough to depress anyone.

Why couldn't funerals be more uplifting and evangelistic? What would any saint of the Lord really desire for the loved ones who were left behind? What had they prayed for in their last tearful petitions to the Lord? Wasn't it for the salvation of their families and friends? And what better place for the Lord to fulfill their last request than at the funeral service, where family and friends gathered to pay their last respects? What better opportunity?

John determined to change the format and content of his funeral services. The music would be more uplifting. The sermon would reach out to the audience with the good news of life in Jesus Christ, here and now, while there is still breath within us.

With two churches to pastor, his first opportunity soon presented itself.

There was only one drawback. While the deceased person was a devout member of his church, one of the family members was a Methodist minister. The family requested that both he and John take part in the sermon. This made things a bit more complicated. John felt certain that Pastor Horney would talk about the loved one already being in heaven, and he would then appear to be contradicting the minister by saying the saint was in the grave, waiting for the resurrection morning. Feeling burdened by the potential disaster, John prayed that God would take full control.

The day of the funeral dawned sunshiny and clear. John spent most of the morning reviewing his notes and praying for the Holy Spirit. Then he dropped by the fellowship hall and checked on the women who were preparing a meal for the family. The luscious aroma of sweet potato pie, coconut cake, and homemade rolls wafted out of the kitchen. If food could lift the spirits of a grieving family, then this family would definitely be uplifted today!

He checked to make sure the organist had the music under control, then sat down in his office and prayed silently. Soon cars began to circle the parking lot as people began trickling in. Pastor Horney arrived, and the two men shook hands and reviewed their notes. John could tell that this man had been in the ministry for a while and was far more experienced than he with funerals. So far, so good. Now, if he would just avoid the subject of when a person goes to heaven.

He needn't have worried. Pastor Horney spoke about the glories of heaven but didn't attempt to say when a person arrived there. John spoke of the necessity of following the Lord with the whole heart in order to be prepared for the coming of Jesus.

Afterward, John rode with the funeral director to the graveside service, and Pastor Horney followed behind in his brand-new Mercedes. Once they were by the graveside, the two ministers visited with the family members for a few minutes, then John read 1 Corinthians 15:51-55, and Pastor Horney closed with prayer.

John sighed with relief as the group headed toward their cars to return to the church for the meal. He had sensed God's presence and felt as though hearts had been touched by His grace. When the last hand had been shook, he turned toward the waiting funeral car.

He saw Pastor Horney eyeing him, as if trying to make a decision about something. "Would you drive my car back to the church?" the man asked as he tossed the keys to John. "I want to talk with you about something."

"This is a brand-new Mercedes. I've never driven one like this.

Does it operate the same as a Chevy?" John joked.

The older man laughed and got in on the passenger side. They had no sooner hit the highway than he turned toward John. "We have a 20-minute drive back to the church. So you have 20 minutes to tell me why I should be a Sabbathkeeper."

John immediately eased up on the gas pedal. He wanted to stretch out every mile he could. To this day he doesn't remember exactly what he said, but he was aware that Bible texts were coming easily to mind.

When they eventually arrived at the church fellowship hall, Pastor Horney turned to him and said, "I would enjoy getting together sometime to study the Bible. Do you have time?"

Did he! For months John met on a weekly basis with the minister, his wife, and teenage son. He watched them wrestle with the decision to change from Sunday worship to Sabbath worship, a decision that involved not only their job but their retirement and future employment as well. In tears the minister confessed that for 30 years he had instructed his congregation to turn to the back of their hymnal every Sunday and read aloud part of the fourth commandment, knowing that it had been misapplied.

"For 30 years," he said with deep contrition, "I knew I was teaching a lie."

God's truth eventually won, and John had the privilege of baptizing this man and his family. Wanting to make sure this baptism was done right, John lowered the former Methodist minister almost to the bottom of the baptistry.

"I thought you were trying to drown me!" Horney accused him later.

"I just wanted to make sure all your sins were covered," John grinned.

The two men hugged each other. A desire to follow Jesus completely had united them closer than brothers.

The minister's son went on to a Christian academy. Years later, after John had become an evangelist, he conducted a series in the church where this young man and his wife and child lived. It made his heart glad to see that they were keeping the faith and attending

Sabbath services on a weekly basis. Another family tree had been changed by the beautiful truths in God's Word and by His almighty grace. His truth was marching on!

Chapter 23

In 1978, the same year that Dale got a break, John got one too. It happened on a Sabbath morning as he readied himself to stand in front of the Grasonville congregation to preach. One of his church members walked into the office. "Did you know that Joe Crews is here?" he asked.

"Oh, really," John commented. "Do you suppose he'd like to take the pulpit this morning?"

Joe Crews was the director of Amazing Facts, one of the fastest-growing radio and TV ministries in the denomination. His books were best-sellers, and large crowds flocked to hear him preach. John had the utmost respect for this saint of the Lord.

"Shall I ask him?" his elder asked.

"No, let me speak to him."

John hurried down the corridor and found Joe standing in the foyer, talking with someone. "I'd be honored if you'd preach this morning," John said after greeting him.

"No, John, I came out to hear you." He smiled and shook his hand warmly.

The sermon that morning was about a potter who took a lump of clay and formed a teacup. He put the cup in a fiery oven and baked it, then took it out and painted it—sprayed it with fumes before popping it back in the hot oven. John compared the experience of the teacup to our lives. God is the potter who molds us. Sometimes it hurts. He paints our lives with beauty, but we find ourselves writhing in agony over broken relationships, diseases, and trials. Were it not for these moments in the fiery oven, however, we would not become a perfect creature in Christ. "'We glory in tribulations,'" he read, "'knowing that tribulation worketh patience; and patience, experience; and experience, hope: and hope maketh not ashamed; because the love of God is shed abroad in our hearts by the Holy Ghost which is given unto us'" (Romans 5:3-5).

John related instances when God had molded his character, and how he gained precious insights through what he thought were the worst experiences of his life. He concluded with 1 Peter 4:12 and 13: "'Beloved, think it not strange concerning the fiery trial which is to try you, as though some strange thing happened unto you: but rejoice, inasmuch as ye are partakers of Christ's sufferings; that, when his glory shall be revealed, ye may be glad also with exceeding joy.'"

A few days later the phone rang. It was Joe Crews. "John, I would like to invite you and Crystal to join Amazing Facts as an evangelistic team. Would you both come into the office and talk with me?"

Would he! It had been his dream to be an evangelist and reach large crowds of people with the messages of Daniel and Revelation. It was what God had called him to do. Not that he hadn't been happy as a pastor. He had enjoyed his congregation immensely and felt that God had used him to enrich their lives. But he knew that God ultimately had another plan.

And so it was that we found ourselves packing up the parsonage and house-hunting for the seventh time in our married life. John had just turned 29.

God had many lessons to teach us about trusting in Him. I fretted over where we would find a house we could afford close to the Amazing Facts headquarters in Frederick, Maryland. John assured me that God had a thousand ways to provide a home. He suggested we take it to the Him in prayer at the breakfast table.

"But you have a series of meetings starting in three weeks clear across the country, and the conference wants us out within four weeks!" I exploded. "How can we find a house that soon? Good houses at good prices are hard to find." I plopped a steaming bowl of oatmeal a little too hard on the kitchen table, and some of the hot cereal splashed out on my hand. "We'll probably wind up in some dingy apartment." Two tears trickled down my cheeks.

John tenderly took a clean kitchen towel out of the drawer, ran cold water on it, and wiped my hand. "God wants us to be comfortable," he said. "He wants us to come to Him about our desires and needs. Now let's pray. Each one of us can add a sentence or two in the prayer. Tell the Lord what you would like in our new home. Crystal, would you be first?"

I closed my eyes. "Dear Father, You know we need a home away from the evils of the city," I prayed. "You have given council that we should grow most of our food. Would you please help us find a home that has a garden plot and some fruit trees?"

Angie went next. "I would like a house with a long driveway so I can ride my bicycle," she said.

"I would like to live in a place that has lots of nature," Tammy added.

John gulped. So far no one had mentioned anything about what the house itself should be like or how much it should cost. "Precious Lord," he concluded, "You know us better than we know ourselves. Please help us to find a house that we can afford."

Later that night John felt impressed to call the pastor of the Frederick church. Perhaps he knew of a parishioner who had an available house.

"There is a church member who moved to California and hasn't sold his home," he told John. "He comes back every few months, and it just so happens that he is here now. He might consider renting it to you." He gave John the man's phone number, and within minutes John made contact and set up an appointment.

During the two-hour drive the whole family wondered what kind of a house they would find. How would the Lord answer their very specific prayers?

Angie clapped with glee when they drove up a long driveway on the border of a Boy Scout camp. The two girls did high-fives when they discovered that the entire property was surrounded by trees, including three large apple trees loaded with fruit. As soon as John stopped the car, I made a dash to see the garden spot just beyond the fruit trees.

"This is it!" I told him as we headed toward the front door.

"This is exactly what we prayed for!"

"Not so quick," John cautioned her. "We haven't heard the price."

The owner of the house kindly welcomed us in and showed us around the inside of the house. I gasped when I saw the living room. Large windows on three sides of the room framed a beautiful view of the valley below, giving one the feeling of being on a high mountain. A baby grand piano, surrounded by lovely green ferns, took center stage on a Persian rug.

"This is the music room," Mr. Hill told us. "This was my wife's favorite room in the house." His eyes saddened. "She died some years ago. I remarried, and my new wife works in California. I would like to sell the home; I'm asking $150,000."

"We haven't been out of college long," John told him. "I'm sorry, but we just can't swing that amount. Would you consider renting it?"

"Let me think about it. Call me in a day or so."

"If you would rent it, do you have any idea how much you would ask?"

"About $500 or $600."

John swallowed, and I tried to smile in spite of the tears that threatened to fall. I knew we couldn't afford that amount. In 1979, $600 for rent on a minister's salary was unthinkable.

Neither of us said much on the way home. The girls chatted excitedly about the house and how much fun they would have playing in the creek. In the front seat their parents stared straight ahead and were strangely quiet.

Two days later John phoned Mr. Hill. "This is John Earnhardt," he began. "I'm just calling to let you know that we won't be able to rent your house."

"Is $500 too steep for you?" the man asked bluntly.

"Yes," John admitted. "We really haven't had time to save any money yet. College bills took every penny we could earn."

"I understand. Can you afford $400?"

John nearly dropped the phone in surprise. "Would you rent it for $300?" he asked excitedly.

"I would for you," the man stated. "I don't have time to stay around and try to sell it. I need someone I can trust to take care of it. You are a minister, and you should be honest."

It was all John could do to keep from falling on his knees. "Thank you so much! We'll take it."

Three weeks later John left for a series of meetings in Ohio. I had no choice but to pack the house myself and help a husband-and-wife moving team load the truck that the conference sent to move us. The girls and I carried boxes, working from dawn till midnight, then drove two hours and unloaded it by moonlight.

I was exhausted and frightened to be in a strange house up on a hill alone, way out in the country. I knew no one; John was hundreds of miles away; my favorite dresser was scratched. I managed to get one bed put together before the workers left, and the girls and I crawled into it, thankful for a comfortable place to stretch out. "O Lord," I prayed. "Is being an evangelist's wife always going to be like this?"

And then I remembered our prayer about the house. God had given us everything we had prayed for, everything we needed. I need not be afraid. God was there with me, and He would never forsake me.

Meanwhile John was having the time of his life. The little church in Ohio to which he had been sent was situated in a small town of about 300. On opening night at least half the town turned out to hear messages from the books of Daniel and Revelation. At the end of the meetings 25 had made a commitment for baptism, and another 25 for future Bible study.

During the last week of the meetings one of the candidates decided to be baptized outdoors, even though it was January. He and the pastor, along with a Bible worker, decided to check out a small lake out in the country for the ceremony. The three men drove close to the water and parked the car.

"How do we know if this is a good spot?" one of them asked. "There could be a drop-off or sharp rocks."

"You're right," another agreed. "One of us should walk out there and check it out."

It grew quiet in the car as each one pondered the situation. Cold day . . . icy water . . .

Simultaneously John and the Bible worker turned toward the pastor. *"You'll* be the one left with these people. *You* need to baptize them. So *you* should check it out."

The young pastor shook his head. "I don't have any dry clothes."

"There's not anyone here. Take them off!" John encouraged.

"And go out there naked?"

"The baptism is this weekend," the Bible worker pointed out.

"What if someone comes while I'm out in the water?" The pastor was clearly thinking ahead.

"We'll watch for you."

It was true—they had to choose a spot that day or run the risk of losing a candidate who didn't think an indoor baptism would take properly. Reluctantly the very thin pastor shed his clothes, handed them to John, and tiptoed cautiously into the water. He was about knee deep when a man and woman topped the hill and started toward them.

"Someone's coming!" the Bible worker hissed, then turned tail and darted for the car with John right behind him.

The startled pastor dived for deeper water and sank down until nothing could be seen but his head. No one wanted to be recognized. With half the townfolk attending the meetings, they could just envision the next day's headlines.

As John and the Bible worker peered out of the car window, the couple reversed directions and headed back up the hill. So they had seen the pastor in his birthday suit!

As soon as they were out of sight, the two men jumped out and motioned for the pastor to come quickly! He needed no second invitation and literally shivered and shook into his clothes. Two of the three laughed all the way home. The other one's teeth were chattering so badly that you couldn't understand what he was saying, which was just as well.

But his ordeal with icy water was only beginning. That weekend proved to be as memorable as the scouting expedition had been. Sabbath's dawn found him peering out the window at a cold, gray sky. He already knew what the temperature of the water was. Cold. Icy cold. He comforted himself with the thought that all heaven would be rejoicing over this newborn babe who was shedding a life of sin and committing heart and soul to God. A few minutes of discomfort would be nothing in comparison. How long could one baptism take, anyway?

Hours later a large group met on the banks of the lake to witness the baptism. The pastor whispered a few last-minute instructions to the woman, reminding her that she must bend her knees at the proper time. Then the two of them walked slowly out into the water. Unfortunately the rather large woman had forgotten to inform the pastor that she was frightened of water.

After the pastor said a few words, he raised his hand. "And now I baptize you in the name of the Father, the Son, and the Holy Spirit." He then began to lower the woman into the water. But instead of bending her knees, the dear soul stiffened up, and the pastor could not move her.

"Now, sister," he whispered reasonably, "just bend your knees. It will be all right."

"OK, OK," those on the bank heard her reply hoarsely.

Once more the pastor intoned, "I now baptize you—"

Instantly the woman stiffened, and the poor pastor was left to wonder what he should do to complete this ceremony and get out of the cold water. "Now, sister," he whispered again, "it will be OK. I know you're scared, but I won't drop you. Just bend your knees." He could see the crowd on the bank. Some were smiling. Others looked concerned. For a third time he began the now-familiar phrase, "I now baptize you . . ."

For a third time the woman stiffened up, and the shivering pastor had but one option left. He jumped up out of the water and forced his weight down on the dear saint, who was promptly baptized.

Chapter 24

In 1980 Dale Earnhardt became the first driver to win the points championship the season after winning the Rookie of the Year award. That same year John was officially ordained as a minister of the gospel. The ceremony took place in a tent camp meeting in Maryland.

The years passed quickly as the Earnhardt family crisscrossed the United States, holding meetings in Pennsylvania, Texas, Tennessee, Iowa, Maryland, and North Carolina. I home-schooled the girls for two years, but as they grew older both girls wanted friends on a daily basis. John and I could understand. So I stayed home so the girls could attend the Frederick church school. John hated driving off and leaving his little family alone on the hill, but what choice did he have?

Once when he was scheduled for a series in Ohio, he became ill. He had to go. There was no one to take his place, and the church had spent thousands of dollars in advertisements. Poor John could hardly hold his head up. I wrapped his throat with warm cloths and helped him into the driver's seat of the motor home. As he rolled out of the driveway, I prayed that somehow God would overrule the devil's plan.

John declares that the angels drove him to Ohio, or at least helped. He doesn't remember passing through the various states. He only remembers the feeling of relief when he finally reached the church. The pastor gave him directions to the church member's house where he was to park the motor home. He silently thanked God for being with him thus far. By now he had lost his voice and wondered how he could preach the next night.

He phoned the Amazing Facts manager. "Floyd," he whispered

over the phone. "You're going to have to come out here and preach. I can't do it."

"John," he answered, "we're going to pray for you at the office all day. God will work a miracle. I can't come, and neither can Joe or any of the other evangelists. But we have faith!"

The pastor prayed. The girls and I prayed. The Amazing Facts staff prayed. But at 7:00 that night John could not speak above a whisper. His head hurt, and a fever made him sleepy. Somehow he managed to dress and get to the meeting hall. The worried pastor anxiously prayed in a corner as John stood up at 7:30.

Suddenly a feeling of exhilaration that he had never felt before passed over him. He preached for 45 minutes, and then sat down. A sudden wave of sleepiness and nausea returned, and he crept back to his bed. He slept until time to leave for the next meeting, where he experienced the same wonderful but strange heavenly healing that lasted only 45 minutes. Then the agony of a plague returned.

John afterward concluded that if a minister couldn't get his point across in 45 minutes, then he couldn't get it across at all. To this day he rarely goes over 45 minutes in any evangelistic sermon.

■ ■ ■

John wasn't the only one in the Earnhardt family traveling around the countryside. Dale Earnhardt followed the NASCAR circuit, gaining popularity wherever he went.

On one rare occasion John and his dad were able to sit down and watch a NASCAR event together. Everyone in the family knew that James Earnhardt let nothing interfere with a Sunday afternoon race. He had been known to leave company and friends sitting in the den while he slipped out to his truck and turned on the radio so as not to miss a lap.

The anticipation ran high this particular Sunday. It was the Coca-Cola 600 on Memorial Day weekend. Dale quickly made it to the front and stayed there for 64 laps. Top drivers like Irvan, Elliott, and Allison were on his tail like fleas on a dog. After 220 laps Dale had no choice but to pit. In his eagerness to get back on the track, he drove too fast in pit row, and the officials penalized him for speeding.

The crowd tensed. Dale Earnhardt did not take penalties with a smile. His face took on a mask of determination. Greg Sacks now became a problem to him. He wouldn't let Dale pass. Suddenly Greg spun sideways, and the sportscaster began shouting that Greg had been tagged by Dale. It was these little tags that earned Dale the title of Intimidator. The officials were not amused. Dale was penalized one lap for rough driving.

Sitting in the den, James Earnhardt shouted and rolled around in his seat. *Put Dale back a whole lap!* There was no way Dale could win now. John sat back and smiled at his dad's agony. To James, racing was serious business, and Dale had every right in the world to do what it took to win a race.

Dale was plainly infuriated, and seemed even more determined to show the world what he was made of. Every driver knew his temperament and experienced mixed emotions when they looked in their rearview mirror and saw Dale behind them, breathing down their neck like a swarm of angry bees. Now his hours of plucking ivy off the wall while driving around a track made sense. He put the pedal to the metal, and minutes later the sportscasters were shouting again.

"What a battle for the lead! Earnhardt and Ernie Irvan are wheel to wheel! And Earnhardt goes back in front!"

John sat back in the La-Z-Boy recliner and watched Dale fly by the checkered flag, savoring his third 600 win and his fifty-fifth victory. His determination to fight against the odds made the ride in victory lane even sweeter.

That week John wrote him another letter.

Dear Dale,
    I'm going to be in your area conducting a seminar on the book of Revelation next month. I would love to see you. Can you come?
                    John Earnhardt

No reply. John knelt in prayer. "Please, God, touch his life. Help him to see his need of you."

The years continued to roll by. John's grandfather Earnhardt passed away in a nursing home, and not long after his grandmother followed. We saved enough money to buy their property in Misenheimer, North Carolina. It was tough moving from our rented home on the hillside where nature abounded freely. But common sense told us that it would be a better investment to own a piece of land instead of continually renting. It was like coming home again. The familiar grounds where John had once played as a little boy reconnected him to his roots. Amazing Facts didn't care if he lived in North Carolina—location makes no difference to a traveling evangelist. All he needed was to be fairly close to an airport. By now the girls were enrolled in a Christian academy for their high school education, and I was free once again to travel with John.

Now that he was back in the area, John decided to visit his old buddies from school. He found Tony suffering from a divorce. David was on his second marriage. Terry had crashed into a tree while speeding around a curb. The impact broke his neck and killed him instantly.

The news sent him to his knees. If only his friends would have opened their hearts to Jesus years before, they could have been saved from so much misery. He knew beyond a shadow of a doubt that we would have been divorced by now had it not been for the grace of Jesus that had changed our lives. Had he done enough for his friends? Should he have kept after them?

The next shock hit him as he was browsing through a sporting goods store. He really hadn't planned to go in this particular store, but as he was driving by he felt the urge to stop. He browsed for a few minutes, taking time to examine the rows of fishing gear and camping equipment. He was about ready to leave when a male voice asked, "Let me know if I can help you find something."

John looked up to see the same one-armed man he had almost shot when he was a child. Of course the man didn't recognize him and wouldn't have known that John had once stood in the window with a gun aimed at his head while he was talking with Julia.

"I'm John Earnhardt," he introduced himself. "You may not remember me, but I remember seeing you at our house years ago. My parents are Julia and James Earnhardt. Everybody called my father Shorty and my mother Sis."

The man acted surprised and almost embarrassed. The two chatted for a few minutes. John was about to leave when the man extended his one good arm and touched John. "I just want you to know that I'm a Christian now," he said. "God has changed my life."

"And to think that I almost killed that man," John told me that evening. "He would have died in his sins, never knowing Jesus."

"God has a way of intervening," I agreed. "It's scary to think what would have happened to us had we not given our lives to the Master."

Chapter 25

ohn soon learned that evangelism could be hazardous to his health. For one thing, he was forced to ride in the car with pastors who weren't known for driving so one could enjoy the scenery. In fact, more often than not, he found himself clutching whatever he could clutch and pressing his foot against an imaginary brake as they careened around dangerous curves in pursuit of potential candidates for the kingdom of God.

On one such excursion in Virginia he and the pastor were discussing the meetings as they drove through and around steep mountains. He marveled at how the pastor could concentrate on the road and the conversation at the same time, particularly since it had just begun to rain. In fact, he was wishing that the pastor would quit waving his hands in the air while making a point and keep them firmly in the 10:00 and 2:00 positions on the steering wheel.

He was about to suggest that when they approached a sharp curve. Before he could say a word the car began to hydroplane. He could actually feel it leaving the road and gliding through the air. Unfortunately, gravity took over, and it dropped downward with such force that he felt as though his stomach had tried to escape and had gotten caught in his throat, a sensation not unlike the one he experienced when his kids had talked him into riding a monster roller coaster at Sea World. It's amazing how only one word comes to mind at such times:

"Jesus!" both men cried out in unison.

At the name of Jesus a strong angel with heavenly strength flew underneath and caught the car in midair with one hand, and gently lowered it to the earth below. No, they didn't actually see the angel rescue, but how else could that car have landed on all four wheels without driving their heads through the roof?

When the car landed, the two servants of God sat in stunned silence. There were no words adequate to utter. Eventually they looked out the window and became aware of their surroundings. They were in a cow pasture. Some of the beasts stood nearby, chewing placidly and staring intently at the strange intruders who had dropped into their quiet world from outer space.

The pastor cleared his throat, and John got out of the car and opened the pasture gate. Once they had gotten back on the road, he noticed that both of the pastor's hands were firmly on the steering wheel.

It was during that same series of meetings that John's throat began to bother him. Without warning, he would start coughing right in the middle of a sermon. It was frustrating to be standing in front of a hundred people, trying to keep a straight face yet cough enough to scratch the itch and keep his train of thought intact. Usually he kept a glass of water beside his notes, but on this fateful night there was none.

I read his mind and hurried out to find a cup. Unfortunately, the kitchen cabinets were all locked. In vain, I tried to open every door in the room; then suddenly I spied a plastic cup beside the sink. *Probably used,* I thought. But since there wasn't any other container he could drink from, I grabbed the cup and rinsed it several times. Then I filled it with water and took it back inside the auditorium.

Gratefully John began to drink. On the third or fourth swallow he detected a strange taste. *Probably medicine,* he thought. *It would be like Crystal to add something to my water. That's probably why it took her so long.* He gulped down the whole glass and turned back to the audience and his sermon.

But as he opened his mouth to speak, strange things began to happen. Bubbles floated out of his mouth. Big bubbles; huge bubble that floated softly on the air. While one part of his mind was trying to deal with a tickle and bubbles, the other part of his mind was acutely aware of the wide eyes and dropping jaws of the audience.

He turned to the stricken pastor who sat in shock on the front pew. "Pastor," he managed to say between bubbles, "would you kindly take over?"

After a moment's hesitation, the saint of God stood up and continued talking as if he knew exactly what John had been going to say.

John hurried out the door with me hot on his heels. "What is in this cup?" he sputtered as soon as we were out of earshot of the others.

"Nothing!" I said. "I rinsed it out several times."

"Show me where you got it."

It didn't take long to solve the mystery. Evidently the cup had a considerable amount of dishwashing liquid in it. In my haste I didn't notice the clear liquid. A couple of rinses just didn't get it out.

It was easy to explain to the audience what had happened, and everyone got a good chuckle out of the whole experience. But it was a long time before John would go anywhere without carrying his own personal cup.

Chapter 26

Two years after the fall of Communism, we packed 10 large boxes of Sabbath school supplies—Bibles, projectors, and any other useful items we could think of—and flew to Bulgaria. Freezing rain pelted us in the face as we deplaned and walked into the tiny airport.

I never realized how bad conditions could be in a country until I paid a man a dollar a box for helping us unload. The excited man had never seen so much money. He jumped up and down, waving his $10 fortune in the air.

The customs agent eyed the money and tried to figure out how he too could get some. Most people didn't tip anyone in customs. As the boxes went through the line he eyed them suspiciously. "What are in these boxes?" he demanded.

"Presents for churches and children," I told the man.

"Presents," he said slowly, holding out his hand.

Giving a customs agent money would be interpreted as bribery in America, so it never occurred to us to do so. A Bulgarian pastor entered the room and began to explain in Bulgarian our mission. But the agent simply shook his head and told them to leave.

We had no idea what was happening. All we knew was that those months of planning and cutting out felts suddenly seemed in vain. We were herded out to an orange van and told to get inside. As we rode through the busy streets of Sophia, the two men in the front seat seemed engaged in a deep conversation. A large woman sat beside me and smiled at me. I attempted to ask questions, but all anyone would say to me was "No problemo." John said nothing. I assumed he was praying—or was he in shock?

For two hours we continued to ride. All I could think about was the time and money I had put into buying and making Sabbath school supplies for the little ones. The church had no money for supplies, so the children usually played outside during Sabbath school. Bulgaria had been 40 years with no official church services on Sabbath. The children had been forced to attend school six days a week. Those who were caught not attending on Saturday were taken away from their parents.

The youth class in the Grasonville church that we had once pastored decided to be a part of the Bulgarian mission project. They made angels and stars on sticks for children's classes and bought gifts and books. I had cut out several sets of felts, and John had raised money for a projector for the Bulgarian pastor he was to work with. And now it was all gone. We had nothing to work with. Nothing to give.

I stared out the window at the cold, pelting rain. I didn't know where I was going or how long it would take to get there. Eight weeks! Eight weeks of being in a country where I could not understand one word! Tears spilled out my eyes. I quickly turned toward the window so the woman beside me couldn't see my face. Some missionary I had turned out to be!

Evidently I hadn't turned quickly enough. The woman saw the tears and distress in my eyes. She too had experienced pain and hardships. She grabbed my head and crushed it to her ample chest and began singing. I couldn't make out the words, but the melody was plain enough: "Jesus, Jesus, Jesus! Sweetest name I know. Fills my every longing. Keeps me singing as I go."

It was as though God spoke to us. His message was simple: "You did not come to give them *things;* you came to give them *Me*. These people have been through 40 years of persecution and poverty. They need to be reassured that I am with them."

I looked at John. He smiled reassuringly at me in the gathering darkness. It was enough. Together we would do the job we had come to do. The city of Blagoevgrad would never be the same. God could bless with or without visual aids. I straightened up and hugged my newfound Bulgarian sister in Christ.

What an adventure we were about to experience!

■ ■ ■

John and I were taken to a small apartment on the fifth floor of a high-rise. Of course there were no elevators. The apartment, like all the others in the building, had two bedrooms, a small kitchen and living room, and a toilet closet. We later learned that the church treasurer, Nada, and her husband, George, lived there, but had moved in with friends so we could have some privacy. We also learned that the Bulgarian people had had their land taken away from them during Communism and had been forced to live in high-rise apartments where the government could control their water and heat. When Communism fell, the officials burned all the deeds to the property so that no one could prove which and how much land they owned.

Since we could speak no Bulgarian, a young university student, majoring in English, was hired to be an interpreter. His name was Peter, and he came over every day to review the sermon material with John.

Peter showed us around the city, taught us the money system, and often visited with us in the homes of the people who came to the meetings. By now the brethren at the Bulgarian church headquarters had managed to get the boxes of supplies from the greedy customs agent. The people were promised a Bible if they attended at least two weeks.

However, Satan would not give up his territory without a fight. While the 750 visitors were sitting in the auditorium, workers overhead hammered on boards during the sermon and dropped nails on the people's heads. It took many visits to officials before that was stopped.

Then a Bulgarian woman, who was considered to be demon-possessed, began to parade to the stage in the middle of the sermon each night. Once there, she bowed and then danced until the ushers could escort her off the stage. She disturbed the meetings so much that the ushers began looking for her at the front entrance to turn her away. Each time she managed to slip past them.

John and I had never encountered these types of attacks in the United States. Every day we knelt in prayer and implored the Lord to work a miracle. John was sure that there was no clay the Lord could not mold. There was no mind so dull that it could not be made brilliant by the love of Christ.

The following evening the "crazy lady," as most people called her, entered the hall. The ushers grabbed her by the arms and attempted to carry her out, but she collapsed to the floor. Then she slithered like a snake down 30 steps and up on the stage right after John had begun the sermon. As she attempted to dance, John took her arm. She immediately slithered to the floor again. John put his hands on her head and began praying out loud. She struggled and squirmed on the floor, but he held her fast and prayed even louder.

Suddenly she stopped moving. John finished the prayer and released her. She stood and faced him with a look of intelligence in her once-dull eyes. Then she turned and went to a seat, where she sat with rapt attention throughout the rest of the sermon.

The next evening the ushers were prepared and waiting. When they approached her, she informed them that she had come to learn and would not interrupt again. She kept her word, and at the end of the series when the Bible lessons were graded and the Bibles awarded to the people, "crazy lady" received a standing ovation from the crowd. She had done all the lessons and gotten all the answers correct. She stood with the others and was baptized, a new creature in Christ.

One evening as John and the pastor left the building, two men approached them. "We would like to visit with you," they said. The pastor set up an appointment for the next day at 3:00 p.m. and wrote down the address. The following day they drove around the area for more than an hour before they found the address in a dark, narrow alley. No one was there. The two men, who had intended to kill them, had gotten tired of waiting and left. Once again God had intervened.

Meanwhile, I spent my time visiting with people and teaching the minister's wife, Zory, how to teach Sabbath school. I scheduled a class for the children in a side room during Sabbath school so I could tell them Bible stories using the felts, but the adults would not hear of it. "We want to hear the stories too," they told me.

So I taught the adults and children each Sabbath, using felts and other visual aids. The truth dawned on me that a whole generation of Bulgarians had grown up never hearing the familiar Bible stories of David and Goliath, Daniel in the lions' den, and other stories that tell about a God who lives in the hearts of His children.

When we boarded the plane to leave Bulgaria, tears streamed down our faces once again, a mixture of joyful and sad—joyful because Peter, our interpreter, had been baptized, along with "crazy lady" and hundreds of others; sad because we knew that we probably would never see these dear sisters and brothers in Christ again.

The song was true. "He keeps me singing as I go."

Chapter 27

In addition to Bulgaria, Amazing Facts sent John and me to the Philippines three times. Sometimes we found people in bamboo huts, sitting around watching a race on a color TV. "You kin to Dale Earnhardt?" they would ask hopefully. John would always laugh and say: "I am when he's winning."

I went with him everywhere. I gave health talks, played the piano, and greeted people. In Cebu the brethren asked me to give a devotional talk to the workers.. John had always been the one to do the public speaking. I was amazed that the Philippine people wanted to listen to anything I would have to say. With only one day's notice, I knelt by my bed for hours, pleading with God to give me something to say that would glorify His name

John knew I was nervous about the assignment, and he prayed that God would give me peace. The next morning I stood in front of the hundred or so teachers and pastors. He says he had never seen me speak so freely. I talked about the God who wanted to take our burdens. I told stories and read Bible texts, concluding with a story that brought tears to everyone's eyes. Then I sat down, relief written all over my face.

The Philippine Union president stood up and smiled. "How many of you were blessed by Sister Earnhardt this morning?" he asked.

Everyone raised their hands. "Good!" he said. "How many of you would like Sister Earnhardt to come back tomorrow and speak with us again?"

The room erupted in clapping. John sighed. He looked over at me. Two preachers in one family. Well, at least he'd have someone to take over if he got sick.

Something extraordinary happened before the third trip to the

Philippines that prevented me from going with him. By this time Angie and Tammy had both graduated from college, Angie with a degree in nursing and Tammy with a degree in psychology.

Tuition bills had kept the family budget tight for years. Now both girls were college graduates, married and on their own. It was December. We had paid the last college bill. John and I kicked up our heels and celebrated.

Then I started feeling extremely tired. "My body cycle isn't regular," I told John nervously. "I'm late."

He looked at me, not comprehending what I was saying. *Why do women always talk in circles?* He must have thought. Out loud he said, "Don't you feel like going to your family's Christmas party today?"

"Yeah, but we need to stop at the drugstore on the way back."

John nodded. So she needed medicine of some sort. *Why didn't she just say so?*

Later that afternoon I stood holding a tiny stick in my hand. After explaining my mission to John in detail, I walked into the bathroom to perform the simple test. John waited anxiously.

After a few minutes I returned in numbed silence. He took the stick from me. Positive! He would be a daddy for the third time! He grabbed me in his arms and swung me around the room. No matter that both of us were more than 40 years old and already had grandchildren. It had been 25 years since we had brought our last bundle of joy home from the hospital. We were going to be parents again!

Not long after this, our youngest daughter phoned us. "I have a surprise," she teased. "I bet you can't guess what it is!"

"You're pregnant!" I guessed.

"How did you know?" Tammy couldn't believe her mom figured that out over the phone.

"I have babies on my mind," I answered.

Being pregnant was exciting, but being pregnant at the same time as my daughter was even more exciting. The two of us talked about babies, shared maternity clothes, exclaimed over all our body changes, and shopped for baby furniture. It was one of those golden memories that I will always treasure. At least when

Tammy phoned to complain about water retention or changing hormones, I could say, "I understand, dear." And Tammy was sure that I did.

Chapter 28

So John went to the Philippines the third time—and left me at home. There was no way he would take me thousands of miles from my doctor. My feet were swollen, and I kept going into false labor. He prayed often that God would lead us. Traveling around the world with a small child didn't seem practical. Should he stay in evangelism, or should he settle down and shepherd a church? He thought I might find being a mommy again at 40-plus a bit harder, at least physically.

When he returned, he heard that Dale was signing autographs in the High Point, North Carolina, mall. John decided to make one more attempt to rekindle their friendship. He walked in just as Dale looked up from signing a woman's T-shirt.

Dale smiled and waved. There were about 300 people waiting in line to see him, so John waited a few minutes. Suddenly Dale looked at his watch. John hurried over just as two men from NASCAR whisked him away from the crowd. He paused, waiting for John to catch up.

"Dale!" John exclaimed. "It's so good to see you."

Dale's smile was warm as he shook John's hand. "Hello, John Earnhardt. Good to see you, too." He looked tired. The two men moved about impatiently.

"Dale, we're going to get mobbed here in a few minutes," one of them warned.

A crowd of people surged toward them. The men grabbed Dale's arm before he could say another word and pulled him away. Later John heard that Dale had earned $8,000 for two hours of signing autographs in the mall. He also learned that his fame had cost him his privacy.

■ ■ ■

After much prayer John and I decided to accept a church district and become a pastoral team again. Physically both of us needed a break from traveling. We had jetted across the country with Amazing Facts for 13 years. Miraculously, the pastor in the church where our older daughter, Angie, was a member, decided to accept a call to Alaska. With John being the pastor of that church, we would be a 20-minute drive from Angie and a four-hour drive from Tammy.

Angie was delighted. She worked in a Christian hospital as a mom/baby nurse. She helped us house-hunt, then picked out a good doctor to deliver her sister. We had been in that district a little more than a month when my water broke—six weeks early. I phoned Angie at work.

"You'd better come on in," she advised me.

"But I'm not in labor yet."

"Mom, your water has broken. The baby has no protection. Come on in."

I nodded at John, picked up my suitcase, and headed for the door.

"What are you doing?" John fussed as he took it from me. "Let me carry the heavy stuff." We hurried to the van. John helped me in and then started the car.

"Where is my suitcase?" I asked, looking around.

John sheepishly got out of the car and went back inside, leaving me in the front seat, chuckling. Were all expectant fathers this nervous, even if it was the third time?

We did have reason to worry about the baby coming early. Fortunately, Angie was still at work. She and four other nurses met me in the parking lot of the hospital. They talked excitedly as they prepared for the delivery. After false alarms all night and all the next day, the doctor decided to induce labor on Saturday morning. The anticipation was driving everybody crazy.

Angie's husband, Keith, brought their 2-year-old son to the hospital for the big moment when the little boy's aunt would be born. Little Robby walked around the delivery room, asking every few minutes, "What's Memaw doing up on that table?"

Then Keith, who also worked in a hospital as head of the Biomedical Department, decided that John wasn't in any shape to coach me, so he volunteered for the job. "I'm a good breathing coach," he told me. "Can I stay in here and help?"

"No!" I shot back. "You just want to hear your mother-in-law yell in pain."

Keith appeared to be wounded. "How could you even think such a thing? I really am good at this." He was silent for a moment. "I won't look at anything but your face," he promised. "Can I stay?"

The fire in my eyes said it all. "No!" I ordered. Maybe this natural childbirth idea wasn't such a good idea. All I knew at the moment was that everybody was laughing and in such a good mood, and I was tired, in pain, and wanted to scream. But I had made up my mind that I would not scream, and I would not take any medication. Unlike my other two deliveries, I would be awake and fully in control. Angie had had Robby without medication, and the doctor had patted her after the delivery and said, "You're a real woman!" Now this same doctor would say the same thing to me. He would say it, or I would choke it out of him!

Ashamed and shocked at my rising temper, I prayed, *O Lord, what is happening to me?* Aloud I said, "Angie, do other women get mean on the delivery table?"

Angie nodded. "You'd be surprised at some of the things we hear coming out of the mouth of otherwise sweet and mild women. It's OK. Pain and hormones will do that to you."

All the nurses were personal friends of Angie's, and it was unusual to have a nurse's mother in the delivery room. Three or four of them walked around, chattering excitedly. Meanwhile, Angie stood on one side of the bed and breathed in the rhythmic pattern with me. With all the noise and distractions going on, I couldn't seem to focus. I felt as if the birth of my baby had become a theatrical production. Of course it wasn't, but when a person is not good at tolerating pain and is fast using up her last ounce of energy, nothing is in perspective.

At last I sat up. "Out!" I ordered. "Everyone out except those who have to be in here!" The look in my eyes sent Keith, Robby, and two nurses out the door. John almost went too, but I grabbed him by the shirttail and pulled him back. "You have to endure every bit of this with me," I told him emphatically.

Angie and Tammy had been born in the days when fathers weren't allowed in the delivery room. He had never seen anyone in this much pain. Tears and sweat mingled in rivulets down my head, and I clinched my teeth and squeezed the life out of his hand every time a contraction hit. Feeling rather useless, John continued to hold my hand, though it was quite painful. All he could think of was the TV shows he'd seen in which the man stood beside the woman and encouraged her to breathe. So every few seconds he said, "Breathe, Crystal, breathe."

That worked all right for two hours, but at the pinnacle of pain I was panting as hard as I could pant. I had heard John say "breathe" about all I could stand. "What do you think I am doing?" I almost barked. Then I felt bad for speaking so sharply. Poor guy! He didn't know what to do.

"I'm sorry," I whispered through my tears, then another contraction hit and I whimpered, "Just imagine what it would feel like pushing a five-pound sack of potatoes out—"

"Mom!" Angie said sharply. "We all get the picture."

"It's coming!" Dr. Cook shouted. "Push! Push!"

By now all the nurses were standing over me urging me to push. John was yelling "Push!" and for the life of me I couldn't move. I was so exhausted I felt as though a knife were ripping me apart. I fell back and cried, "I can't push anymore"

"Get the forceps," the doctor said.

His words sent a chill through me. "No! You will not use forceps on my child's face!"

The doctor nodded to the nurse to go ahead, and she reached for the silvery instrument that in my mind had the power to disfigure my child. Summoning all my strength, I pushed with all my might, nearly coming off the table in the attempt.

Then everyone was cheering and clapping. The doctor was smiling. John was crying, and Angie was laughing. The doctor placed the tiny bundle on my belly. "If I knew a threat of forceps would move you like that, I would have done it sooner," he grinned at me.

I held the tiny, red-faced girl tenderly and looked in her eyes. A new life. A new little person who I had waited so long to meet. "You are beautiful, Carrie Ann Earnhardt," I whispered to my baby daughter. "Happy Birthday! And welcome to our family."

John and I watched as our firstborn child gently took her sister and suctioned her mouth and cleaned her up. "Nobody is going to stick my sister but me," we heard her tell one of the nurses.

I waited for Dr. Cook to tell me that I was a real woman, but he said nothing as he stitched me up. "Dr. Cook, I'm waiting for you to tell me what you told Angie when Robby was born," I prompted.

"And what did I say?"

It sounded childish now, but he stood waiting, so I answered, "You patted her and told her that she was a real woman."

"Did you ever think otherwise?" he patted me on the arm, then turned and left the room.

John enveloped me in his arms. "You're about as real as they get," he told me. "And don't you forget it."

It was a day to remember. As the nurse wheeled me out into the hall, a whole roomful of church members greeted us. I wanted to pull the sheet over my head and hide. Then I envisioned them sitting there for hours, praying for a safe delivery. My heart melted with gratefulness. John greeted them with all the parental pride bestowed upon the human race. How good God had been!

Jesse John Allen Rutlege was born three months later to our daughter, Tammy, and her husband, Shannon. Every family get-together now promised to be most exciting, hilarious, and extremely noisy.

Chapter 29

By the time Carrie was born, Dale Earnhardt's success in racing had made him a familiar household name. Footage from races was seen on television each week. His picture was a steady diet of every sports page in every newspaper in the States, yet he maintained an elusiveness that fascinated the world. It was hard to tell if he was shy or just very private. He went through a dry spell during which he won no races but stirred up enough trouble on the track to make sure everyone knew he was there.

Once he said, "I've never thought about being the best or greatest, not even when I started out in what amounted to jalopies back in the mid-1970s. I just wanted to drive a race car, like my daddy."[1]

His love for "just wanting to drive" put him back in victory lane with a grin on his face that told the world that it couldn't keep a good man down. Even his competitors had to admit that Dale was a force to be admired.

Ned Jarrett, a broadcaster and Hall of Fame driver, said, "From early in Dale's career I've said if there ever was a natural-born race driver, he is it. He just seems to have an uncanny ability to do incredible things with an automobile. He can save them when they're so far out of shape it's amazing."[2]

At times he was the man in black with a cool stare and a chilling grin that no one wanted to see in their rearview mirror. One driver attested to that fact after Dale sent him spinning off the track. He was heard declaring that he would "beat the ——— out of Dale" if he could ever catch him.

On July 4, 1993, at Daytona Beach, Florida, Dale led 110 of 160 laps. On the last lap he pinched Kenny Schrader into the wall.

Kenny said later, "I got my nose in there the last lap, and Earnhardt kind of wiped it for me."[3]

His son, Dale, Jr., saw a different side of Dale's character. He wrote, "This man could lead the world's finest army. He has wisdom that knows no bounds. No fire could burn his character; no stone could break it. He maintains a private existence, one that shelters his most coveted thoughts from the world . . .

"His friendship is the greatest gift you could ever obtain. Out of all his attributes, it is the most impressive. He trusts only a few with this gift. If you ever break that trust—it is over. He accepts few apologies. Many have crossed him, and they leave with only regret for their actions. In every result he stands as an example of what hard work and dedication will achieve. Even his enemies know this."[4]

After the birth of Carrie Ann, John met Lois Tyler. Her husband, Carl, had been a professional race car driver in NASCAR's beginning. After giving his heart to the Lord, he had been baptized after learning about the Sabbath. Although he had died some years before, Lois continued to go to the races and witness to the drivers. She saw Dale in the pits on a weekly basis. Concerned over his unapproachable, gruff image, she said to him, "Dale, it's OK to be known as the Intimidator when you're behind the wheel, but you need to be nicer to people."

Dale smiled at her. "Lois, would you like to go with me to victory lane?"

"Dale made a real effort to reach out to people after that," Lois now says. "Stories began to leak out about him visiting children in the hospital and giving money to pay for a church parking lot."

Since Lois was considered to be a "legend in racing," NASCAR sponsors called on her to sign autographs and to make appearances. She decided to use these opportunities to witness for the Lord. Neither Lois nor John were impressed with all the fanfare that went with racing. NASCAR almost seemed to make its own denomination. Although Sunday was thought to be a holy day, they worshiped and prayed before each race, then proceeded to knock each other around on the track, praising God for enabling them to win.

John and I began to plan how we could get a Bible course into the hands of the drivers and race car fans. With John's guidance, I wrote a tract that compared a race to the spiritual race we all must run (1 Corinthians 9:24, 25). Lois included it in the packets of literature she gave out by the thousands each week.

It was about this time that James Earnhardt's eyes began to bother him. He decided to have a cataract operation. The doctor told him that he must first have a physical. It was then he learned that he had cancer. The doctor immediately set up radiation treatments. He had walked into the doctor's office in March, but by June he was too weak to stand.

Julia rallied to his side. They had been through so much together. She had loved him, she had hated him, and now that death seemed certain, she realized they must put the past behind them. They had to forgive each other and spend their remaining days together in peace. She had completely given up alcohol years before when he had had the truck accident. She had made a bargain with God then: "Save my husband, and I will never drink again!" God had honored that prayer, and she had kept her side of the bargain.

During one of his frequent hospital visits to see his father, John asked the doctor, "What do you think caused this cancer?"

The doctor didn't hesitate. "Your father has cancer because he continually poisoned his body with cigarettes."

James was listening from his bed. At that moment he wanted a cigarette so badly. But they didn't allow smoking in the hospital. He had always wanted to quit. Had talked about quitting many times. But the sad fact was that cigarettes were addictive. He couldn't stop on his own. He had been a slave, and nicotine had been his master. He had deceived himself into thinking that he could quit when he was ready. And he would do it one day. But "one day" had never come. Now it was too late. If only he had listened years ago. The old saying that cigarettes were like nails for a coffin was really true. Only this time the coffin would be his. "Dear God," he prayed, "what have I done?"

Day after day, month after month, Julia stayed by his side. She bathed him, fed him, and sat by his side hour after hour. James had never been a communicator, but the look in his eyes said it all. One morning he reached out and patted her hand. She knew it was his way of saying, "I love you."

As in times past, whenever a crisis came the family pulled together. John went to his father's bedside. He had lost more than 100 pounds. He was but a shell of his former self. Gone was the father who sped around the racetrack, so daring and fearless. He had seemed such a giant then. What could John say to him now? He wanted to yell, "Dad, I told you to quit smoking! Why didn't you do it for me? Why didn't you do it for Carrie, who will never know her grandfather! Your death is so senseless!"

He knew enough to know that anger was a natural part of grieving. Well, so he was grieving. But he was supposed to be the strong one here. He was not only the son; he was a minister. As a minister, hadn't he stood by countless people on their deathbed? It had never been easy, but it had never been this hard, either.

The house was quiet. The oxygen tent by James's bed made little gurgling sounds. The two men were silent for a while. "Dad," John finally said, "the Lord loves you."

"I know, John." His voice was labored and slow. "The Adventist pastor has been to see me. I just want you to know that I've given my life to the Lord. I'm ready to go."

John squeezed his hand. His father closed his eyes and slept. He'd lost the battle with cancer, but John felt comfort in the fact that he had won the race for eternal life.

It was a cloudy day when they buried him in the Methodist cemetery in Gold Hill, North Carolina. John conducted the funeral service. At the end of the graveside rites, clashes of thunder and lightning scattered most of the group who had gathered to pay their respects. I waited in the car with Carrie Ann, now 3 years old, while John said his final farewell to his father.

Julia stood beside him. She felt empty, as if her heart had been yanked out of her body. It was so hard to close out this chapter of her life. She looked around and took in the sites where she had buried the rest of her family—her mom and dad, her brothers and sisters. How many times had she said goodbye to someone she loved? Even her best friend Rachel rested in this cemetery.

I'm old and alone, she thought. The thing she dreaded most of all had come true. Although three of her children lived in the same county, they had families of their own and little time to spend with her. James had been a quiet man, but his very presence had filled the house. Now it would be a living tomb for her. As she walked to the waiting line of black cars, the rain began to fall, first in little droplets that mingled with her tears, then turning to a downpour that matched the torrential fears that roiled inside her.

---

[1] Tom Higgins, *Dale Earnhardt: Rear View Mirror* (Champaign, Ill.: Sports Publishing, Inc.), p. 130.

[2] *Ibid.,* p. 131.

[3] *Ibid.,* p. 146.

[4] Dale Earnhardt, Jr., *A NASCAR Legend, A Father Just as Special.*

Chapter 30

We pastored the churches in Westminster and Anderson, South Carolina, for six years. Although John enjoyed his work, his first love was evangelism. When the call came for him to be a conference evangelist for North and South Carolina, we prayed for God's direction. All the signs pointed back to the road. We both knew that it would be different with a small child, so we bought a motor home.

On February 18, 2001, the two of us sat in front of the TV, watching the race taking place in Daytona, Florida. As usual, there were several wrecks. One driver tapped another driver from behind, spinning him into a third driver, who was sent tumbling through the air, flipping twice. Everyone held their breath until that driver walked away from his car.

On the last lap the crowd became ecstatic. Waltrip, who drove one of Dale's cars, was in the lead, with Dale, Jr., second, and Dale, Sr., third. It seemed as if Dale, Sr. had decided to protect the two drivers in front of him, preventing anyone else from passing. Suddenly his car wiggled slightly, veered left, then took an abrupt right before being hit on the passenger side by Ken Schrader. Then it barreled into the wall, nearly head-on.

While they cruised down victory lane, Waltrip and Dale, Jr., had no idea what this victory had cost.

Dale's wreck didn't look half as bad as the earlier one that the driver had walked away from. Besides, the TV announcer was focusing on the win, not on Dale, Sr., who was last seen being carted off in an ambulance. It was time to leave for the meetings. John turned off the TV and left for the meeting hall.

Five minutes before he stood up to preach, a man rushed into the meeting hall and handed John an announcement that Dale had died from a severe injury to his head. Stunned, John spent a few minutes talking about Dale and asked the audience to pray with him. It was the first time he had ever had difficulty focusing on a sermon.

The story of Dale's death saturated the media. The tragedy hit the front page of the New York *Times* and most newspapers in the country. Almost immediately thousands poured out to Dale Earnhardt, Inc., with flowers and cards. Grown men cried for days. Others openly declared that they'd never go to another NASCAR race, because their favorite driver wasn't there. Vigils and memorials were held with thousands in attendance.

The place of Dale's burial had to be withheld from the public for fear of overzealous fans who had been staking out the cemetery where his father, Ralph, was buried. Services were held in Kannapolis, North Carolina. The following day, in Charlotte, 2,500 invited guest attended Calvary church, and scores of uninvited guests paid their respects outside in spite of temperatures in the 20s.

People couldn't stop talking about their fallen hero. *Sports Illustrated* printed a special commemorative issue, and *People* honored him with a front cover story. They all felt that Dale was more than just a legendary driver.

As John held meetings around the country, some attended because of the Earnhardt name. In one meeting a woman sat on the front row every night because, as she put it, "John, you look so much like Dale, it makes me feel comforted to look at you."

John wondered if Dale had ever given him a second thought since their meeting in High Point at the mall. Ironically, an e-mail from a man he had baptized in Maryland years before answered his question. He wrote, "I am very sorry about your family's loss, and I hope they are doing well. I got to meet Dale at Dover a year after you and Crystal were here. He treated my friends and me like royalty when I told him that I knew you. He asked how you and your wife were doing."

Later Lois told John that one of the driver's wives always put a Bible verse in each car before a race. Somehow Dale didn't get his that day in Daytona. He refused to start the race that day until he had been given his Bible verse. It read, "The name of the Lord is a strong tower: the righteous runneth into it, and is safe" (Proverbs 18:10).

Sometimes people ask John to talk about Dale. This is what he says:

"I'd rather talk about the big race. How do we win? There is only one way. Jesus must be in control of the wheel. This is the secret to the Christian's race to victory lane. We are to live for Christ with the same passion and intensity that Dale Earnhardt put into racing. He never gave up. He said, 'I want to give more than 100 percent every race, and if that's aggressive, then I reckon I am.'* He lived each day preparing for a race and focusing on that finish line.

"God does not care if we come in first or last. He just wants us to finish the race and cross over to victory lane, where Jesus is waiting with arms open wide."

---

*Dale Earnhardt, in a 1986 article about his aggressive racing style.

Chapter 31

*D*ale's death caused John to reflect on his life. The two of them had so much in common, yet they were worlds apart. Both came from homes where racing was as ordinary as taking a bath. Their fathers wanted nothing more than to fly past that checkered flag and coast to victory lane. In their early years they both ate and slept with racing on their minds. Neither could boast of coming from rich homes, but at the time of his death Dale Earnhardt had turned his passion of racing and other business ventures into more than $40 million.

Dale never lost sight of his dream. He lived and died doing what he enjoyed the most, and he passed that legacy on to his children, just as his father had passed it on to him. Dale, Jr., was driving around the track the next week after Dale's funeral. Maybe it was therapy for him. Maybe it was torture. Whatever it was, he followed in his father's footsteps and bore the name Earnhardt with pride. Dale, Jr., has worked to keep Dale Earnhardt, Inc., going.

John visited DEI in the spring of 2002. Dale's brother, Randy, graciously allowed John and his family to go behind the doors to the private world of Dale. There he toured the first-class restaurant that Dale had built for his employees and for private parties. He touched the leather seats, knowing that Dale had once sat there, and gazed at the deer head decorating the wall, knowing that Dale had probably shot it. Hunting was almost as big a passion to Dale as racing.

John listened to the employees talk about how Dale spent hours in his office signing things for fans, and how the Intimidator spoke to each employee every time he walked through the doors. He browsed through the shop where Dale and his mechanics had worked on the Number 3 car. Then he watched as his little girl, Carrie Ann, climbed into Dale, Jr.'s car and sat proudly behind the wheel. He didn't let her stay there too long; that legacy was not hers.

Nor would it be the legacy of any of his children or grand-children, if he could help it. He wanted them to enter a different kind of race, the race where Jesus would be behind the wheel. He wanted the treasures they earned to be laid up in heaven, where Jesus would be waiting. He didn't want the glory and ado-ration of people; he wanted the crown of victory from his heav-enly Father.

When May rolled around, John and I and Carrie Ann went to see Julia. We found her in her favorite spot by a window, watch-ing the bird feeder. She exclaimed over the various birds that vis-ited her new "restaurant."

"How are you doing, Sissy?" I asked, using my mother-in-law's nickname.

"Better," she said. "My heart and diabetes bother me some, and my leg hurts all the time. But the Lord has let me live this long for a purpose." She looked earnestly at the two of us. "You know, Mother's Day is coming up soon. I wonder if I could request a spe-cial gift."

"What do you want, Mom?" John asked.

Julia leaned forward, and there seemed to be a sparkle in her eyes that hadn't been there before. "I want a large-print Bible."

John looked at his mother in astonishment. A slow smile spread across his face. "Sure, Mom; you know I'd be happy to buy you that."

"It just hurts my eyes to read with my glasses on, and I thought that if I had a large-print Bible I could read it more easily. I know the Lord has left me here for a reason," she repeated. "I just need to know why."

We visited for a while, then hugged her goodbye. Julia followed them out to the porch and stood there watching until we had driven out of sight. Neither of us knew if it was the imprinted pic-ture in our minds of her standing there alone, or if it was her

Mother's Day request. But both of our eyes were wet.

The nurse's prayer, uttered so long ago in the back of a tavern, had been answered more completely than she had ever dreamed possible.

The tavern where John was born

James Earnhardt in a micro midget

Lineup at the racetrack

Little John in his daddy's car

Julia Earnhardt, ready to race

James Earnhardt (number 25) in a race

Getting assistance after an accident James, who owned several racers, is "OO".

Practice always brought a crowd of observers.

Julia Earnhardt with her first husband, James Fatata

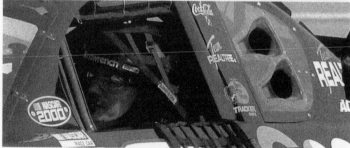

The most famous car in the world: Dale Earnhardt's #3 at Rockingham, North Carolina

"The Intimidator" behind the wheel

Dale Earnhardt salutes fans in Charlotte, North Carolina.

Indy 1999. Father and son wave as thousands of fans cheer them on. The legacy continues.

A reflective Dale before a race

Dale and Lois Tyler. Lois, a
Seventh-day Adventist and
"Legend of NASCAR," told "The
Intimidator" that he needed to
be nicer to people.

Dale Earnhardt

Dale in Bristol, Tennessee

Dale and Teresa in Bristol,
Tennessee

Lois Tyler and Kerry Earnhardt

Dale, Jr., winning popularity,
following in his father's footsteps.

A father and son share an
emotional embrace after Dale,
Jr., won Winston race in
Charlotte, North Carolina.

Legendary driver, Lois Tyler, with Dale, Jr., in New York, August 2000

Lois Tyler with Dale at the "Million Dollar Race," the last race he won

Dale celebrates his last win.

Dale's last victory before he died

Dale and Teresa celebrate the final victory lane.

A jubilant Dale at Talladega, Alabama, in 2000, the last race he won before he died.

John, Crystal, and Carrie Earnhardt stand in Victory Lane winner's circle at Lowes Motor Speedway.

Two famous cars: Father and son ride side by side March 2000.

Lois Tyler and John Earnhardt ride in parade before a race in NASCAR, who does all it can to remind the crowds of Dale Earnhardt, "The Intimidator."

Dale seems to be saying, "Oh, no!" as he looks at car. Dale, Jr., and pit crew look on.

Micro-midget race car built by John's dad for John to use in the children's races that took place before the main racing event. It hadn't run in 45 years. It was restored by John's son-in-law and will be in a July 4 Parade in Faith, North Carolina.

Besides preaching, John also uses radio and television to get the message out.

Because theirs is an on-the-go ministry, Carrie's is an on-the-go education, and the Earnhardt home school goes on the road, as well.